FIRESIDE

THE EDIBLE CONTAINER GARDEN

Growing Fresh Food in Small Spaces

MICHAEL GUERRA

A Fireside Book
Published by Simon & Schuster

FIRESIDE
Rockefeller Center
1230 Avenue of the Americas
New York, NY 10020

FIRESIDE and colophon are registered trademarks
of Simon & Schuster, Inc.

Designed by Bookwork
Edited by Charlie Ryrie

Manufactured in Singapore

10 9 8 7 6 5 4 3 2 1

Library of Congress Cataloging-in-Publication Data is available

ISBN 0-684-85461-9

To Julia, Xavier-Miguel, Alejandro-Luis, and Joaquin-Angel,
who deserve a better, greener, more edible world.
Eat what you grow where you live, and take control.

CONTENTS

FOREWORD

No food in the world tastes better than that you've grown yourself, organically. And there's no greater thrill than harvesting your own produce. When I saw my first row of peas thrusting through the soil I squealed with delight. I'll always remember it as a magical and inspiring gardening moment. Every time seeds push themselves through the earth I experience the same wonderment as I did that first time.

As shoots unfurl, flowers open and pods and roots swell, the excitement intensifies. Nothing beats pulling your own baby carrots fresh from the soil, unearthing the first new potatoes or crunching crispy leaves within minutes of cutting them from the plant.

My first attempt at food production consisted of two tomatoes and a runner bean lodged between two attic windows in West London. Twenty-two years ago we moved to Devon and I was able to make the most of an acre of ground. Few modern gardeners are so lucky. Reality is a small space with rigid boundaries.

However restricted and awkward your space may be, this book shows you how to transform it into a highly productive plot. Side by side with common sense and comprehensive information about the how and why, you are encouraged to revel in the joy of growing food and to indulge your imagination – both in what you grow and the way you grow it. Immensely practical, the book gives us the facts we need – what to grow, when and how to grow it.

If you're concerned about where your food comes from and how its grown, the best solution is to grow it yourself. This book shows you how to use organic methods, however tiny your space, to produce the highest quality food you've ever eaten. It relates your food growing efforts not only to your backyard , roof or steps but also to the bigger reality so that you can garden in tune with nature instead of battling against it. It's the first book which enables us to do so successfully in a tiny space, and to regain the seasonal anticipation and excitement stolen from our lives by the supermarket syndrome. Above all, it encourages you to enter the magical world of growing your own food, to nourish your body and soul wherever you live.

Carol Klein, September 1999

PREFACE

Most people would have looked at the little back garden, ten metres by four, and immediately written it off as a place to grow food. Yet, with little money and not much experience of practical gardening, Michael and Julia Guerra turned this unpromising site into a powerhouse of abundance.

Julia had a bit of gardening knowledge, but Michael hadn't so much as sown a seed when they decided to start growing food. But he did have design skills, partly from his background as an engineer and partly from a permaculture design course. Design skills are helpful but most important is taking your time to think about what you're going to do: in their impatience to get growing, Michael and Julia spent much of their first season wishing they'd done things differently, and spent time the the following winter deciding how to change the lay out. The actual change only took them one weekend's work.

Their regular work of growing the food is pretty minimal too. There's no need for digging and weeds scarcely get a look in. Gardening takes no more than four hours a week on average. Julia has been known to come home from work, look in the garden for a job that needs doing to help her unwind from the office, and fail to find anything that needs doing!

The back garden is fairly secluded, but there are also small growing spaces to the front and side of their house which are in public view. The Guerras approached these areas with caution fearing the response of very conventional neighbours. But they eventually all got to like the edible jungle that advanced round the side of the house! Fruit, herbs and vegetables mixed together in a way that resembles a natural ecosystem are no less beautiful than flowers. It's a less conventional beauty, but a meaningful one.

Julia and Michael's garden has a very special feeling, and it feels much bigger than it is. Any kind of edible gardening is worth it for this feeling, even if the produce is nominal. But what Julia and Michael grow is far from nominal. In only their third year of gardening they calculated that their food bill during July to September was down to £3 each! And you'd be hard put to get the same freshness, purity and variety any other way.

The garden has also been a great inspiration to many people. It has featured on television and radio, in newspapers and magazines, and is mentioned in various books. But this is the first time that all the knowledge and experience which Michael and Julia have gained in creating the garden has been put together in one place. I hope you will enjoy reading it, and enjoy creating an edible garden in your own little space.

Patrick Whitefield, 1999

A small edible garden
can be just as
decorative as any
ornamental one...

No space is too small to grow food. Whether you live in a house, apartment or studio, in a high rise or on a houseboat, you can enjoy delicious, fresh and healthy food right where you live. You can choose to grow tastier varieties of fruit and vegetables than you could buy in any supermarket, and spend no more than a couple of enjoyable hours a week in the process. If you have enough room for a few ornamental plants, grow some of your own food instead and you will still have something beautiful to look at.

This book describes how you can take advantage of whatever space you have and make it productive. It also shows how growing food will give you a strong sense of empowerment, closeness to nature, a real sense of the seasons, and a stronger awareness of life.

Closer to nature

Sadly, many people today have lost the close connection to nature and the land which was once common to everyone, and feel they lack the basic skills of growing food for their families. But this need not be the case. Take a moment to stand by your back door or balcony. Imagine your view full of beautiful leafy plants dripping with the morning dew, long beans and brightly colored squashes dangling from every support, strawberries for breakfast, edible flowers buzzing with insects, an early apple to take for lunch, fragrant herbs to flavor supper, and perhaps even a bunch of ripe grapes for dessert on a trellis overhead. All that is possible, even in the smallest space.

You can grow food anywhere that gets a bit of sun. Your plot could be horizontal, sloping, or vertical. People grow food on roof gardens and in trailers, on stairways and windowsills. You may have a balcony high in the air or a tiny enclosed sunny courtyard. If you have a room that gets so hot in summer that you have to live with the curtains drawn, grow sun-loving food outside the window and benefit from the edible shade. Whatever your space, you can use it.

There seems to be an unfortunate general belief that growing food is difficult, time-consuming, heavy work, and even expensive. For gardeners who buy masses of equipment, live miles from their plot of land, and who double-dig the ground every winter, this may be true. But if you grow food in containers and raised beds right where you live, it is easy because no digging is involved, you need very few tools, and it takes only a moment to give your vegetables the extra bit of loving care needed by confined plants. Also, a small site means that, with careful planning, you can create an edible garden very quickly. And because gardening is such a popular leisure activity a huge industry has been built around it, so there is a vast range of containers, structures and planting material available in garden centres and nurseries to help ensure that your gardening experience is a productive one.

From plot to paradise

If you are gardening in a small space you will need to be more inventive and more adaptable than a gardener with a larger area. Think of your plot as a growing volume, not just an area of ground. See whether you can transform your vertical surfaces into

productive growing spaces using trellis, stepped containers, and hanging baskets. Or you may be able to create more vertical growing spaces with fencing or by building an arch or a small pergola. Use stepping stones or herb-planted paving instead of paths if you don't need to move a wheelbarrow. Build raised beds and use containers where ground-level planting is impossible. Integrate your garden with the house by building window-boxes, filling your kitchen with herbs on sunny windowsills, or extending the house into the garden by placing small seats where there is the maximum fragrance, and fruit within easy reach. If your garden gets very hot in summer, plant for shade, using fruit trees to protect your salads for example, or trailing squashes to protect the roots of your sweetcorn. Your house and garden can become an edible paradise.

Whether you want to start by growing just a few tasty herbs and vegetables in pots, an attractive fruit tree and some edible flowers, or to turn your whole growing area over to food production, there are three clear stages in turning any dream into an edible reality: Survey, Design, and Implementation.

Survey

First you need to survey your site and your family. What do you like to eat? What would you like to try? How much food would you like to produce? How much time and energy are you willing to spend, and how much money? Some of your preferences may be regulated by your site, which has its own opportunities and some limitations: it is a particular size, with certain existing plants and features; it has a particular solar aspect and a range of microclimates, special places, and natural paths. It will lend itself to growing some plants with ease but some may struggle.

Make a list of the plants that offer you the best value, using the information in Chapter Three to help. If you are planning some permanent beds make sure you include a balance of roots, summer and winter vegetables, salads and leafy greens so you can rotate the crops each year to keep your soil fertile. Plan for companion planting and growing a succession of crops. This book will provide you with the decisive information you need.

Design

Spend a few evenings and wet weekends designing your project on paper. Even if you think you can't draw, the process of getting ideas onto paper at the beginning of a project can prevent a lot of wasted energy further down the line, paying dividends in terms of higher yields and efficient use of time, space and money.

The design process is actually very straightforward, the most important factor of all is location – even if you are only going to plant a few containers with food plants, you need to put them where they will have the best chance. Tender plants may need protection from the heat of a summer's day, as well as from frost. Design to overcome the problems of a windy corner, or a shadeless site. If you are investing in a structure, make sure it will support a number of plants. Make sure that you can obtain water easily: run an extension hose, or better still instal a rainwater barrel close to your plants. Make sure plants which are growing close together actually require the same amount of irrigation – don't grow cactus with lettuce!

Remember that you will be generating plant material, both from kitchen and garden. This is not waste, it is a resource! Allow room for a composter or a worm bin so that you don't lose fertility that has to be sourced from elsewhere – even a tiny garden can be at least partly self-sustaining. And leave space somewhere in the garden or close at hand to store tools, trays, pots and compost.

Implementation

Once you have decided what you are going to grow, and how and where you are going to grow it, you can transform your growing space into a productive system. To get the most from a small space, you will almost certainly need to make some structures so make a list of all the materials you will need – containers, compost, wood, nails, screws and so on – and split any construction work into projects that will take, say, half a day for two people. Try to obtain materials from sustainable sources, ahead of time, so that you have everything ready. Choose attractive containers that suit your personality as well as being functional. Plan your tasks so you can work quickly and efficiently.

Whatever your gardening space and style follow basic planting rules, for example making sure any perennial plants and trees are watered well beforehand, and planted in well prepared holes. Spring and autumn are the best times for perennial planting and winter is best for construction, but if you are building and planting in the summer, start early in the day to prevent you and your plants from overheating.

Once your garden is established, winter is also the time to plan for the coming seasons, and order annual herb, flower and vegetable seed. It's a good idea to club together with a neighbor or you will probably have more seed than you can use.

You can green your corner, however humble, and your first steps may inspire others towards a vision of edible greenness, wherever they live. Although this book is directed at everybody with access to any growing space, whether they live in towns, villages, suburbia, on the roads or on waterways, I hope it may also encourage the dream of green cities. Urban dwellers everywhere can realize this vision from their own back doors, taking some of the stress out of city living.

Chapter One

GETTING STARTED

Gardening is like learning to cook, start with the basics and with practice your menu will increase...

Corn and squash
Traditional companions grow
side by side in this narrow yard
garden in California

Know your space and know your needs. Garden design is the art of turning what you have into what you want, in this case a productive space. The techniques of gardening in a tiny space actually have several advantages over a traditional approach: if you choose to grow in containers you will have far greater flexibility and increased visual variety compared to gardening in permanent beds. You can start small with a few herbs or salads, and gradually expand to embrace a wider range when you're ready. Gardening is very much like learning to cook: start with a few basic techniques, use these as your building blocks, and with practice your confidence will increase and your repertoire grow.

Each garden space is different, and every gardener. If you are new to gardening, and not sure how you will take to it, it is best to start simply with just some herbs in the kitchen, and some salads in a deep tray outside the back door. Or you may decide to take a low-maintenance approach and begin with a few containers permanently planted with fruit trees or perennial herbs. More experienced gardeners may be keen to plunge straight in and grow as much produce as a space will permit.

The process of setting up and maintaining a productive plot can be split up into four stages: Survey, Design, Implementation, and Maintenance. This chapter takes you through each stage by looking at the key principles of garden design and how to care for any productive garden. If you know what to look out for, and gradually build upon a few sound principles, your gardening experience should be a long and satisfying one.

Design Principles

Any successful edible garden must work for your site and provide what you want to eat. But don't let a small or apparently unpromising site put you off from the start as even the most difficult space can offer great growing potential. Did you know, for example, that you can grow soft fruit such as currants and blueberries very successfully in containers? Or that you can grow some salad leaves all year round? Or that you can grow potatoes on a balcony, and an orchard on a roof?

...the main limit to a small garden is the gardener's imagination...

Surveying the options

Before investigating the possibilities that your garden space offers, look at your household: What do you all like to eat? What would you like to try? Who (if anyone) will be interested in helping with maintenance? Send away for seed and fruit catalogs and mark the produce that appeals to you all. How much money are you prepared to spend to get going, and how much time do you have available to maintain your plants? It need not be expensive or time-consuming if everything is well planned from the start, there are ways of keeping even intensive vegetable growing relatively low maintenance. Or you may be happy to establish a fairly intensive system, everyone's requirements are different. And don't worry that an edible garden will prove too much of a tie, it is rarely difficult to find a neighbor who is willing to come in and water and pick produce in return for a share!

Your survey is about making lists, and then shortening the lists by removing unrealistic information. Finally, arrange the elements into some sort of order – this could be based on cost with the

21

cheapest produce, salads and soft fruit, at the top, asparagus beds and automatic irrigation systems at the bottom, or perhaps list in maintenance order with fruit trees at the top and salads at the bottom, or arrange according to seasonal preferences. It doesn't matter what criteria you choose, but ordering the lists in a variety of ways gives you a more balanced view of the elements.

Once you have a clear idea about what you want to grow, survey your site. Don't rush this. Look at the size and shape of your gardening space, but also take the time to walk around and "experience" it in a variety of conditions. Try squatting low to feel the effect of being out of the wind, to gauge the effect of any windbreak. Watch the sun as it curves through the sky, and moves shadows over the site. If some corners seem very dark experiment by placing reflective materials – foil, mirrors or white-painted boards – in the darker areas to brighten them. In a sunny space look at the effect of trellis cut out of cardboard shapes to see the effect of light shading on hot days.

There is no substitute for a good survey, and for good preparation, but in fact a survey is an ongoing process, over years rather than just one or two seasons. You will eventually become intimately aware of your site, all its components, its niches, all the changes in temperament throughout the seasons. It is always better to spend a season or two observing and planning – if you can find the patience – rather than running out to buy trees and expensive containers the first weekend you build up enough enthusiasm, as the same enthusiasm may not survive to correcting the mistakes! And try to involve all your household in the design as many hands will make light work when it comes to getting the garden going, as well as planting and harvesting!

The best start, particularly if you are a beginner, is to spend the first year trying a few annual vegetables in different places to see which fare best. This is a very interesting exercise in any case, as positioning can make an astonishing difference to the health and vitality of plants, and the knowledge you gain from such trials could save masses of effort later. Gardening is all about experimenting – don't be afraid to try things, or innovate, but bear in mind the limitations of any structure, or the fact that plants may not yield well if you try to grow them in extreme conditions.

A very small garden is obviously not suited to crops or techniques used in larger spaces, but there are certain principles that hold good regardless of the scale of the garden. It makes sense, for example, to grow different plants together to provide mutual microclimates and physical support, to grow those plants that need most attention closest to the back door, and to make sure any garden is as sustainable as possible. Although the permaculture model is usually associated with large scale projects, I find it a very useful starting point to address sustainable principles, valid wherever and however you garden.

Supporting roles
Inspired by the permaculture
model, plants at different
levels support each other and
make an attractive group

Learning from the big picture

Permaculture was devised by two Australians, Bill Mollison and David Holmgren, in the 1970s. They observed natural ecosystems and also looked at the impact western agricultural methods were having on the soils and landscapes in their homeland. From their observations they developed a set of sustainable principles that would add to, rather than deplete, agricultural resources, and an ethic concerned with balancing the genuine needs of people and the earth.

It is surprising how successfully you can scale down most themes originally designed for larger spaces. Permaculture ideals cover a multitude of possibilities, and can be used to design everything from a large farm to a window box! For example one preferred permaculture design is a "forest garden" where a diversity of productive plants at different levels support each other and their environment, yet the elements of a forest garden can be scaled to a container the size of a half barrel, with a dwarfing apple, a blackcurrant bush, some chives and parsley, a couple of strawberry plants, and a bean climbing the tree.

Guiding permaculture principles

The relative position of different elements in your garden is really important as space is wasted if you can't get to something. Plant herbs and salads, which you will be cropping most often, in the most accessible places and find ways to use all your space efficiently. Try to train tree fruit along the edges of the site, ensuring that any tender trees are on sun-facing walls, or near the back door so they can be easily protected from frost. While trees are small use the extra sunlight to grow annuals underneath; as they grow use the shade for perennial herbs and salads.

Look at your structures and make sure that you are making best use of them. Don't waste walls or fences but use all vertical structures to support espalier, fan, or cordon fruit trees, or climbing plants, or to provide some shade in a too sunny garden. See that all plants and structures help to improve the growing conditions of their neighbors, rather than detracting from them. There are ways to make each element in your garden multifunctional so a fruit tree provides fruit and shade, or salad provides food and ground cover.

Try not to be tempted to grow too much of one food but grow as wide a range as possible, and keep a good supply of water and compost to sustain your plants. Whatever the size of your garden, try and make it as sustainable as possible by harvesting at least some rainwater, and making some compost. Plants store energy from the sun, so reuse that energy through composting, but also watch your own energy, don't waste it through inefficient design!

Try not to be tempted to grow too much of one food.

Even if your growing space is tiny, you can try to incorporate a variety of niches and species by planting good companions in your containers to improve the health of your plants, or providing a few pots of flowering herbs to feed beneficial insects. Even a very small water feature can be home to useful predatory insects and possibly even amphibians. Achieving a balance is important, try and design your garden so that it can look after itself, staying healthy and productive without having to bring in too many elements from outside.

Designing on paper

The techniques and strategies that you adopt depend on your survey, but the basis for any design is a plan. Don't be daunted if you aren't confident with pencil and paper, or have never tried before; the plan is for your reference only and can be as beautiful and as detailed or scruffy and minimal as you like. The only important thing is that it should be to scale. Even if the only space you have is a small balcony, a staircase or a narrow yard, a plan is the best way to start. And there is something very optimistic about dreaming on paper of green leaves and fresh fruits in the darkest days of winter!

First measure your site and lay it out to the largest scale possible on a large sheet of paper (also obtain sheets of tracing paper of the same size). Indicate which direction is North. Mark lines which are immovable: walls, fences, and hedges; also mark any access doors, rainwater downpipes, and standpipes. Then design your garden on a series of tracing-paper overlays. On the first overlay, mark in pencil any existing structures. On the second overlay, mark any plants that are already growing, noting their size. If you have been able to assess them, mark the different microclimates (hot dry, cool moist etc), sunny and shady areas and any soil types across the plot. This provides the basis for the design and provides a record of areas which may need improvement and where plants with specific niche requirements may succeed. Draw your own design ideas on a top sheet of tracing paper overlay.

Once your plot and ideas are down on paper you can develop your design. First look at any dark or cold areas and see if you can brighten them or warm them up. This could be as easy as

painting a wall white or changing a fence from solid boards to trellis, or you may be able to prune a large tree, or even place a mirror where it will reflect some light. Next look at existing trees and structures to see if they could be used for support, for windbreaks or to mark out different areas.

Always keep in mind the direction of the sun. On sunny days see how your shadow, or the shadow of a tree, fence or adjacent building, falls on the ground. You will only have a really balanced profile of your garden after a few seasons, but though some early plantings may be slightly experimental, you will at the very least learn from them, and you may reap very productive rewards. The survey and design process will throw up some areas where only certain elements will succeed. While there is a huge choice of plants for hot sunny areas, even cool moist shady areas have their virtues and could be home to a small pond, along with associated planting, such as rhubarb and mints.

Salad borders
This raised bed was converted from a conventional herbaceous border to become a productive vegetable patch

If there are any spaces that are, or could be, slightly separate from the general circulation in your garden, plan to use them for storage, work areas, composting or rainwater collection – for example, you could place a rainwater barrel on a chest of drawers that serves as a storage for your handtools, labels and twines, or mount a large lid on a water barrel or compost bin and use the area for sowing and propagation.

Never assume that an edible garden will be less attractive than an ornamental one. Even if you don't plant flowers, with mixed plantings and a variety of levels and structures, your garden will turn out to be a lot more decorative than you might at first imagine.

INCREASING SPACE

Don't think of your garden as a flat area but as a growing volume, a sun-facing growing wedge – think in three dimensions! Even a small balcony or roof garden can have extensive growing potential with clever vertical planting. Make use of accessible vertical spaces, and then think about adding extra growing structures such as a fruit arch, or using step-over apples as borders for any ground level beds more than 2m (6ft) long. Pergolas, cane pyramids, strawberry towers, herb spirals, potato stacks, trained trees and fruit can turn a flat design into an undulating 3D landscape, full of colors, textures, and shapes.

Outside inside

Increase space by making your garden feel like an extension of the house, blurring the boundary between indoors and outdoors, with garden-facing rooms becoming indoor gardens. You can use every sunny windowsill for growing popular herbs such as parsley, basil and coriander, or salad greens. Other windows can be used to bring on seedlings such as outdoor greens, squashes and tomatoes, where heat, and not sunshine, is most important.

If you have a conservatory, even a tiny one, you can produce delicate citrus fruits or tender chiles and peppers in summer, and lettuce, endive and rocket can be picked all winter. Use a conservatory to start long-season vegetables like tomatoes and squashes, hardening them off outside on sunny spring days.

If your space and finances don't run to a conservatory, you can easily erect a temporary winter sunspace especially for bringing on seedlings. This insulated space acts as a frost-free greenhouse and allows you to sow long season vegetables such as sweetcorn, chillies and some aubergines, tomatoes and squashes very early in spring. After the last frost, the mini-conservatory can be dismantled or concertina-ed to the wall to allow space for climbers on the wall. I know of one small and highly productive garden which uses a short double-walled polytunnel 2m (6ft) wide and long, 2.5m (8ft) high, giving an astonishing extra six weeks growing time at the start of the season.

A garden can be an outdoor room rather than a separate space...

Many small wall-mounting greenhouse-type structures are now commercially available, but you can make something yourself that is inexpensive and will suit your space perfectly. Simply attach a triangular frame to your sunniest wall, and attach another frame in front of that to whatever depth you wish, then cover with a double layer of plastic sheeting of the quality used for polytunnels. The most satisfactory way to make an entrance is by using battening to make another frame that fits inside the triangular shape, and covering it with plastic. You can attach shelves directly

29

to the wall, or use any kind of lightweight shelving unit, but plants must be off the ground to avoid any potential frost problems. If you have deep frosts at night, you can insulate a sunspace by covering it with a layer of aluminum foil and/or blankets, and you can keep it positively warm by placing gallon jugs of hot water between plants.

Radical coverings

All over the world you find houses built in regular rows, each with small rectangular backyards. If this yard is not already firmly in use for household functions such as drying, washing and storing equipment, temperate gardeners may be able to take advantage of this design by covering the entire space with a seasonal or year-round polytunnel. You may even be able to persuade your family that this is the best use for a yard!

A polytunnel yard may sound a bit radical for most small gardeners, but if you are serious about growing interesting produce it has fantastic possibilities and need not be a difficult or necessarily expensive project – it is easy to pick up secondhand polytunnel frames in many areas, victims of once enthusiastic but sadly failed horticultural ventures, or make your own from hazel or willow. The curving frame poles support the covering in winter, which can be removed in late spring when the frame becomes a support for climbers or hanging baskets in summer. Or you could keep the cover on all year and create a steamy tropical paradise in summer, with tomatoes and new potatoes late in the autumn.

The main drawbacks are the difficulties of rainwater catchment, and the lack of ventilation, damaging to most temperate plants. So you will have to devise some sort of irrigation system using barrels, gutters and pipes, or water regularly and feed the soil – indoor soil becomes depleted and infertile far quicker than soil which is exposed to the natural climate and associated biological activity. On the plus side, if you fix a polytunnel to the back of the house, both will lose less heat in winter, and there will be a beneficial gaseous exchange between house and plants – plants need carbon dioxide to form starches during photosynthesis, releasing oxygen; house occupants breathe out carbon dioxide and need oxygen.

Conserving heat
Whilst the onions dry and peppers ripen red, egg plants continue to grow in this urban conservatory

Alternative spaces

Recognizing a growing space is a matter of opening your mind to the edible possibilities. One beauty of growing in containers is that you do not need any open ground, you can grow on parking spaces, over drainage covers, on grit and gravel, anywhere in fact! It is quite possible to grow 25kg (60lbs) of food in an area the size of one parking space. Think of all the spaces that

Growing in containers gives you the flexibility to grow anywhere....

surround your house: for half of all properties along an East-West street for example, the entrance area and front garden will offer better growing potential than the back garden. Added to which, you probably pass through the area several times each day, and could easily spend a few minutes each trip tending to even quite high maintenance vegetables such as salads, baby carrots, cherry tomatoes or peas and French beans.

Your front garden could be enormously productive without at first glance looking very different from the purely ornamental gardens so popular in front of houses in suburban streets – you could plant an edible flower garden, with roses and daylilies as well as pot marigolds, nasturtiums, and pansies, and add decorative herbs and fruit trees. You could opt for a very formal arrangement including standard and trained roses and a clipped bay tree or two, or even create a decorative potager with vegetables growing between clipped low hedges of fragrant lavender. Once you have built up some confidence, and some rapport with your neighborhood, try trailing a few squashes, planting a block of sweetcorn, or a tub full of rainbow colored chard. You'll certainly make your neighbors curious, and may even get them growing too!

SOIL AND COMPOST

The key to successful growing is to provide your plants with a fertile growing medium. Most limited-space gardens will use some soil as the growing medium, and some compost. If you are growing exclusively in small containers it is not a good idea to use garden soil as it can't maintain its health in pots and tends to compact too quickly.

Soil is a mixture of minerals, air, water and organic matter. It is a highly complex ecosystem, home to huge numbers of worms, insects, bacteria and fungi which live by digesting coarse matter deposited on the soil. Deep plant roots dissolve minerals from rocks in the subsoil, transport it with water up the plant in to the leaves where they are used to make starches from carbon dioxide and sunlight, and proteins from nitrogen and trace elements. Leaves fall and plants die and worms and microfauna and flora incorporate that nutrition into the soil to be available for future plants. Worms support soil fertility and structure by converting organic matter into nutrition, and by maintaining a delicate maze of air and waterways. Plants and soil fauna coexist in an extremely efficient system, able to convert material from one useful form

healthy soil is the key to successful gardening…

into another, using just sunlight for fuel, and gases and minerals as building blocks. Soil is alive, and it must be cared for to maintain its health and the health of everything you plant. The key is to feed the soil, not the plants.

You can generate a living soil in raised beds and even in large containers, but it just isn't possible in smaller containers. So container gardeners must use a growing medium that is rich in plant-ready nutrients, has sufficient drainage to avoid waterlogging, but it is open enough to hold water-soluble nutrients and air at the roots.

Soil in permanent beds

Soil with a good structure consists of mineral and organic particles which bond together into lumps of fairly regular size with a network of spaces around them for drainage, water retention and aeration.

A sandy soil has large particles which don't fuse together easily so there are large gaps and large air spaces between the particles, and water and nutrients drain away easily. Clay is the opposite, with very small particles which stick together very easily so a clay soil is very sticky with few spaces in between the particles for air or for water to drain away; clay soils tend to get waterlogged, and in a drought they dry out into a hard cracked surface that is almost impervious to water – and very difficult to work. Silt soils have medium sized particles, between sandy and clay. The ideal soil for temperate growing is a balanced combination of the three known as loam.

The easiest way to gauge what kind of soil you have is to pick up a small handful and roll it into a ball, or between your fingers. Clay soils are rather sticky and form a hard tacky ball; sandy soil feels rather gritty and doesn't bond together well, whereas a peaty or loamy soil feels soft and silky. A more scientific interpretation distinguishes different soil types by the particle size of their mineral content, and by their acidity, which is measured on a pH scale from 0 to 14.

You can test your soil with a kit from a garden centre. A neutral soil has a pH of 7.0, an acid below that and an alkaline soil

above 7.0. The pH indicates the availability of nutrients – very acid soil locks up some important minerals so they are no longer available to plants, and very alkaline soil locks up some vital trace elements. Most vegetables grow best in a slightly acid soil – aim for a pH of around 6.5.

But whatever soil you start with, you can almost always build it up to have good water holding capacity, good drainage, and a good balance of nutrients. Most soils need little more than the addition of liberal quantities of organic matter, and it is virtually impossible to add too much manure or rich compost. This will gradually improve the structure and provide a food supply for worms and microfauna, also helping drainage and aeration.

Plants deplete the soil of nutrients as they grow, so help the soil to stay fertile by feeding it each time you crop – it is so easy to scatter a handful of compost whenever you cut a vegetable, and leave the roots of leafy vegetables in the ground in raised beds to build humus. Once you have built up soil fertility the best way to maintain it is to limit any digging to the minimum.

Building fertile raised beds

Many small gardens will have scarcely any existing soil to work with, and you may choose to grow entirely in containers. But if you want to make some permanent beds you will probably have to start by removing rubble in a new garden, breaking up paving in an existing one, or transforming grass into soil. When you remove the worst of the rubble or the paving you may find a hard layer (hard pan) beneath. This will have to be broken up as it will prevent natural drainage and cause waterlogging of the soil above. Wherever soil is compacted try to fork over the surface to get some rain and air into it.

Don't worry about removing all stones, they do little harm unless you are planting root vegetables and you can leave a few to anchor any fruit trees. If it's not too weedy grass can be a good resource, you can turn it into loam simply by turning it over to a spade's depth and covering it with compost, soil or mulch.

Once the soil is turned over, weed seeds will be on the surface ready to germinate so you will need to hoe thoroughly before planting the next season. It may be more appropriate to cover the surface with a light-excluding layer to stop weeds from growing or germinating. The easiest way is to use cardboard or folded newspapers overlapping by 20-30cm (8-12in); add a 15-20cm (6-8in) layer of farmyard manure on top of the cardboard and finally a 5-10cm (2-4in) layer of straw or shredded paper. If you

Mulch

Mulching is one of the most effective ways of reducing competition from weeds, it also keeps soils warm, improves water holding, and reduces surface evaporation

don't like the look of it, just add a layer of compost on top. Grow potatoes or squash through the mulch, but leave any light-suppressing covering in place for a year.

If your garden has relatively weed-free soil, build it straight into productive raised beds in autumn. Once beds are constructed place 15-20cm (6-8in) of well-rotted manure onto the beds in winter and allow it to break down. When you start to transplant seedlings into warmed soil in spring, mulch loosely between the plants with straw, shredded newspaper, shredded bark, light manure or compost.

Container Soils

The right growing medium is especially important when growing vegetables in containers. Despite the wide range of container sizes, situations, and plant types, the growing medium does not need to vary by much, but it must be carefully watched to make sure it doesn't compact too much, and constantly revitalized.

Ordinary garden soil is no good for small containers, although large containers such as those containing fruit trees should use a soil-based planting mixture, unless you need to limit weight on a balcony or roof. It is almost impossible to maintain a living soil for more than two seasons in anything but permanent beds.

Soil-based planting mixture

Fruit trees and perennial plantings should be planted in large containers or raised beds in a loamy mixture. If you don't have a supply of home-made compost, there are many proprietary brands to choose from. As well as peat and coir-based products, composted municipal green wastes make an excellent base compost for container growing. Spent mushroom compost, a mixture of peat (*see below*), manure and chalk also makes a good soil improver or basis for potting mixture.

Soil-based mixtures can hold nutrients better than soilless composts, so plants need less supplemental feeding. The soil is also heavier, so gives extra support to larger plants, and stabilizes a large container. One disadvantage is the possibility of harboring weed seeds and diseases, though you can avoid a weed problem if you mulch well after planting.

Many proprietary soil-based mixes are specially designed for supporting plants growing in containers. Most use sterilized topsoil rather than loam as a base, and for the novice gardener these mixes are an excellent starting point, but many of them contain peat along with sharp sand, lime and fertilizer. The mining of peat should not be supported (as it destroys important ecosystems), so seek peat-free alternatives wherever possible. Coir (coconut husk fiber) is often used as an alternative, but it is best to use local resources.

If you or a neighbor have the space to do so, you could try making your own compost A good soil-based container recipe uses 7 parts loam (stacked turfs from healthy soil), 2 parts compost, and 2 parts sand. To each 4.5 litre (1 gallon) bucketful of this mixture add 15gms (1/2oz) of a mixture of 1 part wood ash, 1 part seaweed meal and 2 parts general organic fertilizer such as chicken manure. This mixture acts as a general soil conditioner and fertilizer. Add a teaspoonful of lime if you have used municipal or other proprietary compost other than mushroom compost which is already slightly chalky. Bolster your planting mixture with up to 25% well-rotted manure for all but woody herbs.

Lightweight composts

The major drawback of soil-based compost is weight, making it unsuitable for gardens on roofs and balconies, windowboxes or hanging baskets. Lightweight porous soil additives such as vermiculite (an expanded larval rock) can be used with compost to produce a soil with adequate characteristics. You can use almost any inert, lightweight filler, even plastic packing materials, to provide drainage, and you could use rigid foam plastic blocks to protect your drainage at the bottom. Pots smaller than 20cm (8in) diameter don't usually need filler, as long as their drainage is well protected.

The mixture supplied in peat-free grow-bags is usually well balanced for successfully growing annual vegetables (especially tomatoes, peppers, squashes and salads), and even when the compost in the bags is exhausted at the end of the season it can be mixed with 20% manure and a general mineral supplement such as seaweed meal so that it can be used again. The main disadvantage with soilless composts is that they can dry out easily, and can be difficult to remoisten. They also need continuous feeding in order to stay fertile throughout the season.

A useful starting recipe for a homemade lightweight compost is 25% lightweight packing material, 60% municipal compost, and 15% well rotted manure or compost. Add fertility with lime and trace minerals as per soil-based compost.

This mixture will not be able to maintain nutrient levels as easily as a soil-based mixture, so more regular soil and foliar feeds will be necessary, though this will be a matter for experimentation depending on your location, the size of your container, the design of your garden and so on. Practice really does make perfect, it is surprising how quickly even an inexperienced gardener can come to recognize signs that a plant needs care. Providing you start with a well balanced mixture, you should have no difficulty keeping plants healthy through occasional gentle feeding when watering. You will need to revitalise the soil in your large containers every year, and start again with each crop in small containers.

Drainage is also vitally important in containers, as there is no soil life to maintain nutrients without them leaching away. When filling any container you must protect drainage holes and place pieces of broken clay pots or medium sized stones at the bottom before adding the compost. You can add water-retaining granules to stop pots drying out too quickly but the best plan is simply to make sure you feed and water your containers regularly. Hanging baskets, with a relatively shallow growing depth, and high density planting, are the most difficult containers to keep healthy as they dry out quickly in warm or windy weather, but water retention can also cause problems, so don't be tempted to add a drainage improver such as sand, but make sure that the drainage holes are about halfway between the base of the container and the position of the lowest plant in the basket.

Revitalizing soils

In permanent beds with living soils revitalization is an ongoing process. Providing that you sprinkle a little compost on the soil after you have cropped, and mulch between plants, there is little more you need to do during the growing season. When you are growing productive plants in containers it is a different matter. The soil is soon exhausted and you will need to feed it regularly with liquid feed during the growing season and renew it at the season's end. But you don't need to rush out and buy fresh bags every time you want to replant, you can reuse what you have. If you have any permanent beds it is best to use the used container mixture on your raised beds and make a new batch from scratch, with no such option you can reuse what you have, adding nutrients with some rich compost or manure.

Choosing compost
While hardy fruit trees such as apples and pears are best grown in a soil-based planting mixture, tender citrus fruits thrive best in lighter compost, and must be fed regularly.

Rather than starting with new compost each growing season, you can reuse spent compost several times. If you garden in a tiny space you may think it's not an option for you, but in fact the process is easy and doesn't demand much room. First tip out the container on to a tarpaulin or plastic sheet, and rescue the large pieces of bottom drainage for reuse later. If you are growing annual vegetables, add about 15-25% (by volume) of rich

compost or well-rotted manure; you could add a few handfuls of straw to improve drainage.

If the mixture is for growing fruit and other perennials 10-15% manure is plenty. Sprinkle the mineral supplement and lime onto the mixture, lift up each end of the sheet and roll everything backwards and forwards, mixing up the ingredients and incorporating air lost through compression in the pot. Then you can put the compost back into the pots (remember the drainage) and use it again. You can safely renew spent compost three or four times before starting again from scratch, after this there may be too high a build up of toxic plant root exudations (some woody plants produce chemicals that reduce competition from other plants), disease and a general lack of vitality.

Composting

Compost is the decomposed remains of live organic matter, a balanced soil food made up of those substances taken from the soil by growing plants. Homemade compost costs nothing, and is relatively straightforward to make, turning garden and kitchen waste into a valuable resource. There are three basic ways of recycling your organic waste: hot composting, cold composting, and vermiculture – using a worm bin. Your choice of recycling method will depend on your situation. If you have a small balcony, and grow mostly salads, you are best off with a worm bin. A roof garden may have space for a small compost bin for garden waste as well as a worm bin for kitchen waste. Hot-composting is generally only suitable for large gardens.

A cold composting system consists of a pile of vegetable and animal waste which generates heat slowly and rots down naturally with the aid of bacteria. Cold composting takes about a year so you ideally need to find some space in your garden for two permanent or semi-permanent bins, one for filling and one composting. A simple bin can be made from strong wire mesh placed directly onto soil, the sides lined with cardboard or old

carpet as a form of insulation. A couple of lidded containers at the optimum size of about 60cm (2ft) square and 1m (3ft) tall, could also provide a useful work area for potting up or similar.

Start your compost with a layer of soil then pile up kitchen and garden wastes as they occur, and they will be broken down by a variety of fauna, like wood lice, and beetles, before being attacked by bacteria. It is best to chop coarse material up or it may not decompose fully. When your bin is full finish it off with a layer of soil and then cover it completely with thick plastic or similar until all the material is rotted into a black crumbly mixture. Or a tall cylindrical compost bin with a door at the bottom will allow you to compost continually in a small space. Mix up your waste if you can and fill from the top, while taking compost from the bottom after nine months minimum. These bins work best when placed onto soil as worms love it in there and process your rough compost into something finer.

Hot or aerobic composting is a quicker process, taking 2-3 months to become dark brown and crumbly, but it is best for large gardens, needing a reasonable volume of a balanced assortment of kitchen and garden waste, which is moistened and layered in batches in an insulated container, where bacteria raise the temperature of the pile to around 50°C, sterilizing the contents. Small compost bins are inappropriate for hot composting as they cannot maintain heat for very long.

The best way of composting in small gardens is vermiculture, using worms to eat and digest your organic waste, converting it into 'vermicompost', a peat-like substance. Worm bins are now widely available or you could make your own from a bin and a tub of brandling worms *Eisenia foetida* available from fishing tackle shops. Use any robust container as long as it has a faucet at the bottom to drain the worm pee (an excellent foliar feed when diluted 1:20 with water), a shelf inside to keep worms from drowning, and a ventilated lid to keep out flies. Start the process by placing approximately 1.5 kilos (3lbs) of shredded newspaper in your bin and moistening it with 4.5 liters (1 gallon) water, then adding a handful of worms. Feed the worms with kitchen waste. They don't like very acidic waste, such as citrus or spicy foods, but you can mix these in with blander material. Worms will even deal with small quantities of meat waste, as long as it is added with vegetable material. Add shredded newspaper every so often as a soak, to stop the mixture becoming too anaerobic and smelly. Generally, a household of four would need two worm bins to deal with all their kitchen waste. If worms are not fed, they die.

A worm bin is ideal for making compost in a small garden.

Some people keep a worm bin in their kitchen, but watch out for the summer flies that will surely appear eventually. Empty your worm bin at least twice a year after leaving it for two weeks without adding any material. This allows the worms time to work to the top, from where they can be easily moved to a temporary container while you empty the bin. Then replace the worms in the bin with fresh newspaper bedding and start feeding them again.

Even in a small garden, try and make room for a few comfrey plants, preferably Bocking 14 variety. Pick flowering stems and steep them in water for a few weeks to make a powerful liquid feed, rich in potassium and particularly good for tomatoes. But be warned, the mixture gets very smelly so soak it as far away from the kitchen window as possible!

Using your compost

It is almost impossible to make enough compost, so use it wisely! Fairly rough compost can be used as a mulch and for growing potatoes in a stack. Finer compost can be used as a potting compost with 10% sharp sand added, though it is usually too rich to be used on its own for sowing seeds. Then you should use a blander mixture with 20% sand and some other proprietary base. Worm compost is very rich and should be allowed to stand for a week or two before use. It should then be mixed with drier compost, and used to feed the soil between crops at perhaps a handful per half a square meter.

WATER

When and how much water to use is one of the biggest problems faced by novice gardeners. It is vital to get to know the watering requirements of your plants as different plants have different water needs, depending on factors such as leaf surface area and leaf type, the ambient temperature and humidity, and the strength of sunlight. Some plants grow faster than others, which affects the amount of water they use to transport nutrients from their roots, the faster the growth the more water they need. When plants are small their roots will be nearer the surface where water loss through evaporation is greatest, so seedlings need to be watered more often than mature plants, but if you water too much the plants' roots will not grow deeper to mine for water but will stay on the surface where they will be prone to drying out quickly.

Plants growing in full sun will lose more water than those with some midday shade, but clever planting and shading will adjust local microclimates and so affect the amount of watering you are likely to need. You can keep your watering to a minimum by designing your garden so that large robust plants can shade those that are more tender and thirsty. Also, make the most of ground-cover planting, even in containers: Water loss from plant roots will be reduced, along with surface evaporation, by growing plants so that their leaves touch, and by growing a ground-cover crop such as herbs, perennial or cut-and-come-again salads, or mulching heavily around larger plants.

Until you get to know your garden, test the soil in permanent beds or large soil-based containers several times a day to see if it is moist about half an index finger below soil level. If it is dry water gently at a rate of about 1 liter per square meter/yard. Test again after half an hour and if the soil is still not moist repeat until it is. If you do this test over several days, in different temperatures and weather, you will soon get a feel for how much water your plants need, and before long you will know when to water just by looking at them!

When you are growing in containers you have to accept that your plants will need up to three times more water than if they

Waterwise
A piece of pipe is used in a
permaculture garden as a
watering point rather than
watering plants individually

were growing in a deep living soil. There's no way around this. You can add water-retaining granules but these are no substitute for regular watering. Container grown plants will be easily stressed during hot weather. Crowded hanging baskets grown in full sun will have to be watered at least twice a day, completely soaking the container, as the plant roots will grow to fill the entire basket. During a hot summer you should water your pots daily even after a summer storm, as the containers will not hold much of a reserve, and the heat will soon evaporate any surface water.

Try to grow plants with similar water requirements together – salads with spinach, carrots and beans; potatoes with squashes; tomatoes with marigolds; sage with rosemary and thyme; fruit trees with shrubs. Generally it is better to water annual vegetables little and often, especially in containers. However, trees grown in soil may not need to be watered at all except in drought, and any watering should promote deep root growth. Don't water woody plants near the point where the roots join the stem or you may end up overwatering. They should be watered at their drip-line (the same distance away from the stem or trunk as the extent of their branches), or via pipes that take the water well below the crown. Some plants, including strawberries, are very sensitive to wet crowns, so water them gently between the plants.

Previous page
*Les Hortillonages, the floating
allotments in France, are
intensively planted productive
small market gardens*

Watering Systems

Never be complacent about your rainfall, or about how much water your garden may use. Whatever size your garden, make room for at least one water barrel. Rainwater is much better for your plants than mains water as it is softer and holds nutrients in solution much better.

For most small gardens, all you need is a watering can. Water at the end of the day using a medium rose to allow the water to percolate into the soil before it evaporates, and take account of plants' needs. Shallow-rooting greens may need water several times a day, while young fruit trees should be watered more heavily and less often to ensure their roots go deep. If you use a hose be gentle as heavy watering will turn the top surface of the soil to mud, which can dry out to form a hard crust which will then limit its ability to absorb water.

Few irrigation systems are relevant for small gardens, but if you are growing vegetables intensively in raised beds, or raising expensive fruit trees, you might like to consider a simple system. Drip irrigation uses perforated pipes or porous hoses to allow water to percolate gently into the soil without damaging the soil surface through impact, and you can easily instal some porous soaker hose just under your mulch layer, or you could even use higher pressure drip-emitters. Your supplier will be able to advise you about pipe lengths and water rates, but in general keep pipe lengths short and aim to provide enough water for a day's growth on 15-30 minutes water flow a day. More time will mean more lost to evaporation, while very fast watering will mean more nutrients lost to leaching.

If you are absent from your garden for a day or two – rather than for an extended period – there are ways to make sure your plants are watered. The simplest method is to fill a 2 liter drink bottle with water, punch a 5mm ($1/4$in) hole in the cap and upturn it in the soil (for example in the middle of a salad patch) so the water drains slowly. For my favorite short term watering insurance I sink a few unglazed terracotta pots (with their holes filled) around the garden, and keep them filled. The pots are porous, and when in contact with soil the water is drawn out of the pot through surface tension and osmosis. Large filled unglazed pots also make a pleasant feature to cool a hot garden if you place them where they will catch any breeze, as water will evaporate on the outside of the pot, cooling the air.

Weight restricts water-gathering on balconies and roofs. You may be content to use a watering can and mains water but if you are interested in harvesting some water there are ways to do it. One possibility for a balcony garden is to attach 2m (6ft) lengths of pipe to the wall beside any down drainpipe, capping each off with a tap, and plumbing in to the downpipe to divert some rainwater. A substantial balcony may have room for a water barrel at the strongest structural point.

Roof gardens dry out more quickly than ground level gardens because of the wind. Ingenious (and reasonably low-level) gardeners can devise systems to pump water from water barrels at ground level to a series of small perimeter tanks on the roof, or you may be able to divert some rainwater to wall-fixed storage tanks just below roof level. If such options aren't viable you'll have to use mains water, either from a standpipe fitted to the roof, or use a hose from the nearest downstairs faucet.

Graywater usage

One way of conserving water is to use graywater – sink or bath water – on your fruit trees and shrubs, providing that you are careful with the kinds of soaps, detergents and cleaners you use. Only use biodegradable materials. Don't use graywater in regular irrigation systems because of the particulates it contains, nor straight onto vegetables because of the danger of disease organisms getting into food. Also, if you rely heavily on a graywater system you should analyze your soil fairly regularly as many of the salts used in detergents can build up in the soil and lock up nutrients, so you may need to compensate with a specific soil feeding programme. While graywater can be very widely used in a purely ornamental garden, in an edible garden it is best restricted to perennial plantings, especially fruit trees and bushes, and not on annual vegetables.

...water is precious, look after it in your garden...

CONTAINERS

There are some gorgeous pots around, but don't rush out and buy the first ones you come across, first look at the practical factors such as what you want to use them for, their size and their weight.

At ground level

From recycled sinks and old dustbins to ornate antique stone and metal pots, there are containers to suit every taste and budget, for every scale. Anything that is deep enough *(see pp.148-9)*, robust enough, thoroughly clean and relatively impervious to climate can be used as a container as long as you can make adequate drainage holes. Galvanized buckets are increasingly popular but don't use them for ericaceous or acid composts; half-barrels; wheelbarrows; old baths; catering containers; ice-cream tubs; washing-up bowls, even old car tires fixed to plywood bases can make good homes for plants.

Clay or terracotta pots are many gardeners' first choices. These are inexpensive, they provide a better ratio of container weight to contained soil volume than stone containers, and they have a greater thermal mass than wood, so keep the soil warmer for longer. Also, they are heavy enough to provide stability for even tall plantings, but light enough to move when necessary. And if there is an accident and a clay pot gets broken, the shards can be used for drainage in another container, or smashed small and returned to garden soil to disintegrate eventually. Unglazed clay pots are porous and plants need to be watered more often than in some other materials, and when you first plant a terracotta pot thoroughly water the container itself so that it does not leach too much moisture out of the soil or potting compost.

If you are a cool-climate gardener, make sure your pots are frost-resistant. Pots with wide necks are better than those with a confined neck or Alibaba shape, as there is more room for soil or compost to swell and move as it freezes and thaws. Stoneware pots are less porous and more reliably frostproof than terracotta, though also slightly more pricey. A wonderful range of vibrant colors and shapes exists. Clay pots can also be painted or aged

by brushing them with weak solutions of liquid manure to encourage mosses and lichens to grow.

Stone, reconstituted stone or concrete tubs are much heavier than terracotta, and can only be used for static containers. They also take longer to warm up, but stone pots will last for many generations and need little maintenance other than cleaning them out between plants. Real stone tubs can be expensive, it is cheaper to buy new reconstituted pots and age them (*as above*).

Timber is very cost-effective and attractive for large troughs or boxes. Choose pressure-treated timber (the moisture in the timber is replaced with an oil-based preservative in a large pressure vessel) or seasoned chestnut or oak which will last up to twenty years without treatment, protected by their natural tannins.

After a few years most plastic containers become brittle through exposure to the sun, and are then liable to crack in frost. Recycled plastic containers are now widely available, made from a mixture of post-consumer waste catalyzed together into a strong high-density polymer. Its density means it is extremely water-resistant (all polymers absorb water to a greater or lesser degree) so it should last for many years.

Lightweight containers

If you are a balcony or roof gardener, the first consideration always has to be weight. The lighter the container, the greater the depth of soil you can have, and the more plants you can grow. Your first choice will probably be plastic for weight and portability, but you could use something like polythene lined baskets or make lightweight troughs and attach them to walls. Plastic sacks can make useful growing bags, or use them to line plywood or wooden tubs. Plastic dustbins are usually thrown away when torn or holed, making them unusable for trash but excellent as plant tubs – you can cut them down into low containers or grow stacking potatoes. Recycle cream and yogurt containers for seedlings and small annual herbs, saving larger food tubs for tomatoes, peppers and egg plants.

Relatively lightweight permanent containers can be made with ferro-cement. This is produced by moulding chicken wire into the shape you want and then plastering a fine concrete mixture onto the mesh. It is best for freeform curvaceous containers as undulations strengthen the form.

Containers made of glass reinforced plastic (GRP or fibreglass) should last up to ten years before serious UV degradation, though some cheaper ones will eventually delaminate as a result of water penetration. UV-resistant pigments are sometimes used in the outer gel coat, and you can encourage a longer life by painting fiberglass a dark colour, or by shading containers with planting. Thermoplastics such as polyethylene (PE) and polyvinyl chloride (PVC) have a relatively short life, becoming brittle quickly when exposed to sunlight; there are also some environmental questions about the safety of PVC containers for growing food as some chemicals may leach out of the plastic into the soil.

When you are gardening in a very confined or awkward space it may be best to build simple troughs and boxes to fit the space, line them with plastic, and fill them with a lightweight soil mix, rather than investing in expensive ready made containers. Plywood is a good DIY choice, using softwood battens for the frames. It is lightweight and very longlasting if protected with layers of marine varnish.

...timber, terracotta, stone, cement, plastic, wicker...

The right size

With containers, size really does matter. On a balcony or roof, it is far better to have a few large containers rather than a host of small ones. Large containers allow more flexible use, and plants can be mixed and grown together as in a ground-level bed. They are also less likely to topple in high winds, and have a greater ratio of soil to container weight.

All annual vegetables and most dwarf tree fruit can be grown in containers as little as 30cm (12in) deep. Although many plants will happily send root hairs 3m (10ft) down in a deep, friable soil, if less soil is available a plant will spread its roots horizontally: root volume rather than root depth is crucial for all except root vegetables – unless you choose special dwarf varieties. But if you are looking for maximum productivity, remember that if you have the space to build even one or two small raised beds you will be able to grow more of most fruit and vegetables, more closely together and with less maintenance than is ever possible in containers.

Limiting soil depth does not mean that you greatly restrict your choice of edible plants, but it does mean that you limit plant size. Even if you grow trees in generous sized containers, they will still never attain the same size as the same varieties grown in the ground, for instance an M27 Very Dwarfing apple rootstock will produce a tree of 1.2-1.5m (4-5ft) height and spread in the ground, but you would need an M26 dwarfing rootstock to produce the same size tree in a half-barrel container. Tree fruit designed for open ground will often grow well for several years in containers, but you will have to replant them in fresh compost every other year and feed them more often than a tree on a slower-growing, more dwarfing rootstock as the compost will be exhausted more quickly.

Figs are one of the best subjects for container growth, as long as you have a reasonably sunny and sheltered spot, a south facing corner is ideal. While an unconstrained fig tree can rampage 10-20m (33-66ft) across a wall, destroying its foundations in the process and probably not fruiting very well, if you grow a fig in a container or restrict its root space by burying slabs to create a chamber no more than 1.25m/4 ft deep and wide, the tree can be kept under 3m/10 ft spread, and will fruit prolifically. But some trees will not flourish in containers – black mulberries for example are very sensitive to a lack of water at their roots and need pampering even in ideal conditions.

If you have a windy garden, and can't diffuse it through planting or flexible fencing, you may need to anchor some containers, particularly if you are growing fairly tall plants in them. You can fix guy ropes to stakes in the ground, or rings embedded in a wall, to avoid disaster.

Container hygiene

The golden rule is always to clean your containers thoroughly at the end of the growing season, or when re-potting. And never put containers away dirty. Pots and tools must always be clean, so that you do not spread any disease from pot to pot, or plant to plant. Large containers which have a living soil system will not need much in the way of cleaning as the soil is self-cleaning, providing that it is regularly fed, and not over-watered. With most container composts this is not the case so you must clean pots thoroughly so that they are not pre-infected with some pest or disease. Fungal and bacterial microbes are present in the air all the time, just looking for the ideal place to grow. Some microbes require the presence of a specific stressed plant, specific insect pest, or simply a piece of stressed soil (often waterlogged) that is devoid of other microbe-eating life.

Whatever your containers are made from, the cleaning procedure is the same: first, scrub them out with normal washing-up detergent (use the biodegradable kind); leave them to dry, then wipe them out with a dilute (20:1) solution of hydrogen peroxide bleach – do not use a chlorine bleach. Try and find a cool dry place to store your pots until you need them. It is also a good idea to provide an annual paint or varnish check and touch up on plastic and timber containers.

If you live in an area with heavy frosts, make sure that your plants in clay, concrete or stone containers have plenty of drainage, as a waterlogged container when frozen is likely to crack or even burst, to say nothing of damage to the plant. If clay or stone pots are left unplanted through the winter, if it is possible you should turn them upside down to prevent any frost damage.

MATERIALS

When choosing the design and materials of any structures you decide to introduce into your garden look at what you want to use them for, what they cost, their scale, renewability, and sustainability. Use natural materials such as timber, stone, clay pipes and bricks wherever possible, but also choose according to your abilities and budget – it's no good opting for a very grand scheme if you can scarcely hit a nail straight!

All designs should allow for flexible use so that an arbor, for example, can be used as a supporting frame for productive climbers, offers shade to others and perhaps somewhere to sit. Ideally, you should need only simple tools such as a handsaw, hammer and drill to make up any structures, and it is best if they come apart fairly easily for possible future recycling.

Edging materials

Raised beds should be edged for easy maintenance, good appearance and in some situations to keep in the heat. Stones are

popular, upturned clay or stone tiles, and specally designed edging in fancy designs from rope-edged clay tiles to miniature woven willow fences. Some people keep the soil warm by edging with plastic bottles half-filled with water.

I favor railroad ties (sleepers) in my own small and very intensively planted garden as they are large enough and heavy enough to need only minimal fixing by wiring them together at the corners. They are wide enough to support pots, seedling trays – or small backsides! And good quality treated ties can last for up to 25 years without deterioration.

If you can find hollow cast concrete blocks left over from a building project these make good edgers, their hollows filled with soil and planted with herbs or strawberries. Lengths of

clay drainage pipes are also good, half buried in the soil, but on the smallest sites you will probably need to use boards – recycled planks, floorboards or even new sawn timber if it has been pressure treated, though softwood boards rarely last longer than five years. Softwood should always be painted with a water-based preservative to deter fauna and fungus. Fix boards to posts embedded every 60cm (2ft) along any raised bed.

Traditional edging

Clay or stone tiles with rope edges are attractive to separate different growing areas

Materials for vertical structures

You can create vertical structures from metal or from wood, which is easy to work and the most popular for arches, trellis and pergolas. If you can get hold of them, coppiced poles of ash or chestnut are ideal, as they contain a natural preservative. Bamboo canes can also be surprisingly sturdy and stylish. If you are adventurous – and patient – you could weave your own supportive structure from living hazel or willow, or form living supports from willow, poplar, or hazel staves planted in wet soil.

But if you do opt for a living structure, remember it will take water and nutrients that might better be used for nurturing edible plants.

When putting any structure together, don't bury long vertical wooden supports straight in the soil as they will gradually rot. Instead sink a short treated timber or concrete post and fix your structure to that. A short post can be replaced when it rots without damaging the overall structure (*see p.85*).

...take account of your abilities and don't aim too high at the start ...

Be careful about the way you fix your structure together, a design that depends on a single rusting nail will not last long! If your DIY skills are reasonable fix joints with hardwood dowels, otherwise use screws, bolts and nails. Or lash round poles together with waxed string in the simple and attractive Japanese way. It is a good idea to make sure that any structure can also be taken apart without completely destroying it; you might want to move or adapt it one day.

Recycling

Materials can be a very costly part of any project, but if you keep your eyes open, and your design flexible, you may be able to reduce the costs enormously. See what you can source locally from demolition sites, recycling centers or reclamation yards. Good timber is often thrown out when shops or offices are renovated, you are quite likely to find old garden features in reclamation yards, and in some areas gardeners have brick or stone to spare and are delighted to have it taken away. Decide on your design then see how much of the material you can get secondhand. This will not only keep the cost down, it is a sustainable use of energy and materials.

PAVING AND PATHS

Most small gardens need some kind of hard paving and what you choose can make a huge difference to easy maintenance. If your garden is bigger than a small patio you may also need paths between raised or ground level beds. The shape of any beds may be determined by the materials you choose and by path widths, which need to allow at some points for the minimum turning circles of barrows or wheelchairs. Wheelchairs need a 90cm (3ft) minimum width and turning radius; barrows require 60cm (2ft). Simple walking access can be less than 45cm (18in) wide. Any path or paving needs to be as level as possible.

The best materials

Most small gardens should use a hard material for any necessary paths, particularly if you are growing quite intensively as you will be using your garden fairly heavily. Grass or mulch paths can be attractive but are best avoided in the smallest gardens, for permanent paths choose robust materials such as gravel, bricks, stones, slates, cobbles, tiles, timber decking or concrete pavers. You can use the materials singly or in combination, demarcating various areas or situations.

...to keep a small garden flexible, lay a temporary path for a season...

Light-colored gravel is hard-wearing and reflects light onto the plants. It also allows heavy rain to drain, though with hard use it will get mixed with the soil and become muddy. Cobbles can be laid directly on the ground; slates and tiles require the support of a sand and cement base. Paving slabs should be laid on sand and gravel, but you can leave spaces between them for small scale plantings. Bricks also need to be laid on a bed of coarse sand, or sand and gravel, to aid drainage and provide them with continuous support. If your brick design requires half bricks along the edges, leave them out and plant the spaces.

Over time, any paving will become home to wind-blown weeds, mosses, or self-seeding herbs. Very few of these do any harm, and they are usually easily removed. If your garden was previously home to pernicious weeds such as quack grass or ground elder that spread with runners and will try to emerge at any weak point in the paving, you should probably lay plastic sheeting underneath the sand bedding, before laying the paths. If you have weeds pushing up your paving, the problem will be worse in adjacent beds. However, even ground elder was once considered useful, taken through Europe by the Romans who used it as a salad green!

Many herbs and alpines will succeed between paving, so take advantage of this. Most Mediterranean herbs come from

rocky, limestone areas, which have low rainfall and hot sun. These are exactly the conditions along a sunny path. When laying paving on a sand bed, drop some herb seeds into the top layer of sand between the pavers or bricks. Let the seed sink or swim (seed costs little), as where it succeeds the conditions will be ideal. In cooler areas, allow different salad greens (*see p.131*) to self-sow in the gaps.

Original paths
This larger garden uses recycled material which can be taken up at the end of the growing season and replaced the following year

LOW MAINTENANCE

Easy care
Plant closely together in
troughs filled with well-fed
soil and make use of
companion planting to ensure
good health and productivity
with minimal maintenance

A low maintenance garden is not an unplanned one. To be successful it requires as much initial attention to detail as an intensive vegetable garden. But once the design is realized, you can sit back and relax! You do not have to spend hours every day to make your garden productive. Even with a medium-sized plot of 3m x10m (10ftx 33ft), growing a mixture of fruit, herbs, salads, and vegetables, you can produce a succession of fresh food spending an average of only four hours per week, or less than 40 minutes a day! With a smaller plot, growing mostly perennials in containers, non-cropping maintenance could amount to only an hour a week (or less) during the main growing season. The key to a low-maintenance productive system lies in good planning and preparation and appropriate planting.

Make your garden as efficient as a well-designed kitchen or office so you can move easily from one area to another without having to move something out of the way. Try and make sure that your plants have the best growing conditions possible and that they will grow with a minimum of interference, cutting down on the need for watering, feeding, pruning, training, weeding, and pest control.

If possible, spend a few minutes a day, every day, doing a small task in the garden, rather than leaving everything until the end of the week or month. One excellent routine is linked to harvesting: when you go out to cut a lettuce or pull some baby carrots for supper, instead of just rushing out with a knife, take a small pot of compost and some blocked seedlings along to replace what you have just cropped. Pull the carrots, sprinkle the compost (to keep the soil fed) and plant a couple of seedlings in their place. If you are cropping some catch or inter-crops (*see p. 76*), just take the knife and the compost. It's that easy!

Perennials

Even if you spend a lot of time away from your garden, you can have a productive garden with quite a wide variety of food plants. Instead of concentrating on annual vegetables and maincrop

Pond life
Even a tiny pool of water will
attract beneficial insects into
your garden

salads, invest in perennial plantings of fruits and herbs. Herbs, especially, have great potential as low-maintenance plants, as they are usually hardy and, given a bit of sun, tolerant of poor soils. Fruits require a little more care, you must watch for pest and disease problems during the growing season and crop at a specific time. All plants require some annual maintenance, such as pruning, training, and feeding, but this is not time-consuming. Container grown fruit and herbs will need re-potting every other year, and topdressing in autumn.

Cut-and-come-again salads (such as mizuna, oak leaf and salad bowl lettuces) require much less maintenance than other salads or vegetables. They can be kept trimmed for the table with scissors, growing back a number of times before bolting. This approach to growing is very resource-efficient in terms of time, space and money, it demands the absolute minimum of equipment, within anyone's reach: you may only need a few seed packets, some string for training, secateurs for pruning, and scissors for cropping. This compares well with the space required for the seed trays, compost, and trowel required for growing more intensive vegetables.

Design for low maintenance

When laying out your plot, make sure you can reach all your plants easily. Ideally no container should be more than arm's length – about 60cm (2ft) – away from a path. No bed should be deeper than that either unless you have access from either side, when it can be twice the width. If you don't need paths, and want to plant your plot as closely as possible, then 40cm (18in) diameter stepping stones every 75cm (2$1/2$ft) are adequate, provided that you can still get down to the ground where you need to for cropping and mulching. Permanent paths are usually preferable, because they are easy to keep clear of dirt. Make sure that you can reach all your climbing plants easily from a paved area and avoid walking on any soil, otherwise you will continually have to cultivate it, and digging is not a low maintenance activity!

Raised beds are both labor-saving and the best way of using a living soil in small spaces for intensive cropping (by allowing deeper roots) and minimal maintenance. You can mulch them quite heavily which means longer periods between watering, because the mulch reduces surface evaporation, reduces weed competition, and provides a spongy, water-holding layer that plants can draw on.

Positioning

Whether you are planting in containers or in the ground, place fan-trained fruit against walls, with any other dwarfing trees in positions where they do not throw any shade on each other. If you want to grow some soft fruits, such as blackcurrants, redcurrants, gooseberries or raspberries, place them on the sunny side of the larger trees, with herbs in front of them. Leave a little space

Mutual support
In every planting scheme follow
the golden rule: always help
your plants to help themselves,
then you will be able to grow a
surprisingly wide variety of
fruit and vegetables

between the fruit, where the trees throw shade in midsummer, and use these for cut-and-come-again, self-seeding and perennial salad greens such as claytonia, chickweed, sorrel, chicory and oakleaf lettuce, perennial onions such as Egyptian tree onions and Welsh onions, and the occasional crop of carrots. You can even use the trees as trellis for beans. This is essentially the structure of a forest garden, a planting technique that mirrors a forest edge. A forest garden consists of layers of different height plants to create a productive wedge-shaped planting with small plants on the sunny side and tall plants at the back. Watering will always be necessary if you are growing in containers, even in large ones such as half barrels, but if you are growing in a bed the only maintenance necessary will be mulching between plants, annual pruning, and cropping – the perennial plants can establish deep roots that can source water from deep reserves, and they also protect the annuals from too much sun.

Working with nature

Organic gardeners stress the importance of achieving a pest-predator balance, and this is essential if you don't want to spend all your time fighting slugs and aphids. Low maintenance gardeners in particular must try to work with nature as closely as possible. Although this might conjure up visions of gardening in huge muck-laden beds in large spaces, it is also perfectly possible when you are growing in containers in tiny gardens – flowering herbs such as chives, marigolds and fennel are especially good herbs to attract predator insects, and thrive in containers.

Even if you haven't space for a small pond, a moist spot under some perennial planting, along with some flowering herbs, can make all the difference to ecological balance – and therefore productivity – in your garden. No garden should be an entirely clean and sanitized place, you need some spots for beetles and other insects, some rotting vegetation to encourage beneficial soil fauna and flora. The best way to control slugs is to invite frogs and beetles into your garden, and herb flowers attract lacewings and hoverflies that will attend to your aphids. Even a small water feature such as a tiny birdbath can make a significant difference to your garden, encouraging beneficial birds and insects.

Watering

Some gardeners like to devise ingenious low maintenance watering systems, ranging from pulleys and pumps to old toilet bowls! One popular and attractive design uses a stack of cascading boxes, smallest diameter at the top, each with reservoirs at the bottom. Each container has drainage holes drilled every 5cm (2in) up the sides of varying width boxes 20cm (8in) deep, with the bottom 8cm (3in) filled with gravel, large pebbles or foam plastic packing, separated from the container soil with a layer of netting. The water overflows from one box to the next, the overflow of one box being just above the soil level of the next, with a porous hose between boxes so several containers can be watered from a single point.

If your garden is on a slope, you might devise a system where a rainwater barrel at the highest point feeds a porous hose which winds down the garden to drip water into containers, reservoirs or beds. But however inventive you are, if you are going to be absent for more than a couple of days in an intensively planted garden it is usually easiest simply to ask a friend or neighbor to water during any dry periods.

Minimizing garden waste

Gardens growing mainly perennials generate less plant waste than those that are intensively planted, but much of that waste will be woody and therefore difficult to compost. If you are planting your garden from scratch avoid this problem by choosing fruit trees on very dwarfing rootstocks, and compact fruit bushes, which need little or no pruning.

While the leaves of fruit trees can be left to rot where they lie on beds or containers, winter and spring prunings need to be shredded quite finely in order to compost quickly. Some municipal authorities provide facilities where you can take prunings or brushwood, if this is not possible and you don't have access to a shredder, hammer the prunings until they split open and make a small pile of them in a corner, away from the trees they came from (to reduce risk of disease). If you do not have room for a woody heap, cut the hammered prunings as short as possible and add them to your composting system. Although this is not exactly low

…no garden should be an entirely clean and sanitized place…

maintenance, it only needs to be done once a year. As a last resort, use cuttings as a rough mulch. For small container gardens where most of the garden waste is green (non-woody), it is best to mix it with shredded newspaper and add it to a worm bin or tall cylindrical cold composting bin (see p.42).

Low maintenance gardening is largely a state of mind! If you like regimented rows of plants in neat beds and uniform containers, low maintenance is not for you. But if you are prepared to plant durable perennial plants quite close to one another, your garden could well resemble something wild and natural, even in containers. Close mixed plantings provide a range of natural niches that different plants will succeed in, and provide reciprocal protection. These gardens can be very beautiful as well as productive, with a range of different leaf shapes, colors, textures and fruit blossoms in the spring.

Chapter Two

GROWING SPACES

A garden should add to your enjoyment of life in many uncountable ways…

Good design is the key to the success of a garden – from the simple joy of walking round appreciating that each plant seems happy in its location to the practicalities of whether it is possible to access all parts for cropping and maintenance, or whether it is efficient in its use and scale of materials.

We know intuitively when we look around a garden whether it 'works' or not. The best gardens take the personalities and needs of the gardeners and integrate them with the attributes of the site, forming beautiful and well planned spaces. This is just as true for a tiny food garden, even a balcony or a small terrace, as it is for a large ornamental landscape. Whatever the scale, the particular requirements of any garden's users, together with the possibilities or the limitations of any individual garden will dictate what can be grown and what is likely to succeed, and the character of the gardeners then adds the heart and spirit that brings any garden to life.

...design your garden to express your personality...

Your vision of an ideal garden will be different from mine, which will be different from the next person's. There must be hundreds of thousands of interpretations, every individual will have their own image, and this in turn becomes dependent on the permutations of your own site and climate. However, there are a few general themes for small edible gardens, whatever your particular situation.

Lateral thinking

If your available ground space is minimal, vertical growing could be the solution. If your garden is very hot, you could still grow succulent salads by using taller plants for shade. If you live in a cold area, with a long winter, but still have some solar aspect, then you can either concentrate on hardy perennials and very short season vegetables, or you can extend protection from the house,

with a permanent or temporary conservatory – at the Rocky Mountain Institute in Canada, for example, they successfully grow bananas in a solar heated conservatory, so almost anything is possible! If all you have is a small cold sunless courtyard, then you could look to a Japanese theme or room extension, and use any indoor sunny windowsills, entrances, stairwells or balconies for food.

Your garden should express your personality as well as providing good and varied food, whatever its scale. If you are most comfortable with formal, or more decorative gardens, you can still grow food. You could use fancy containers or turn a small space into a potager with regular shaped small beds of vegetables and flowers, or plan small geometric parterres between controled paths. You could even plan an Elizabethan knot garden with woven edging from herbs or salads filled with edible flowers, herbs and medicinal plants. Follow your dreams, but be aware that formal designs were probably intended to be created on a larger scale so it is usually more interesting to take a fresh look at design.

While there is something appealing about traditional vegetable plots with their serried ranks of cabbages, the best way to make the most of a small space is with more 'niched' integrated plantings. Whether you are growing solely in containers or combining them with raised beds, plant fairly close together, and use plants to help other plants (*see p.66*).

Herb and salad knot
Cut-and-come again lettuces and herbs weave in and out of each other to form an attractive border with a mix of colors and textures, all inspired by a traditional knot garden

Contrasting styles
A New York roof garden
affords stunning views
across the city, while a
decorative gate and picket
fence leads into a more
traditional small
productive plot in
California

Working gardens

A walk around your edible paradise shouldn't be like a tour of an allotment but a sensory feast. Be imaginative with your plant groupings, with the plants you choose, and the way you grow them. Mix edible flowers with fruit, herbs and vegetables, use interesting containers and make original structures.

Look at the needs of all your users. If you have small children for example, although your garden may be too constricting for ball games its proximity to the house makes it a wonderful additional playroom, especially on sunny days, so design with the children's needs in mind. And leave time and space to relax: however small your garden, make sure there is room for a seat – there can be little more satisfying than sitting in your own beautiful garden savoring your connection with it. A seat need not be a grand freestanding affair, it could be a bench forming one side of a pergola, it could hang from a structure or be part of a raised bed, it could have storage for tools underneath, with fruit and vegetables climbing above it – make it large enough for two, to double the pleasure of your garden.

A garden should add to the enjoyment of your life in uncountable ways, it should not be another pressure, or demand for hard labor in an already busy life. In this chapter I suggest a few designs to demonstrate the possibilities of small scale food production, and to explore some of the different themes and strategies that make a garden work. They are meant for inspiration, not to be followed slavishly! In a small space it is

74

particularly important to make your garden work with you, not against you. Keen gardeners may want to develop specific themes further, planting more annuals, training fruit into decorative shapes, or perhaps experimenting with different planting combinations. For them intensive themes like year-round salads may be appealing. Others may just want a few summer vegetables, or to concentrate on fruit, or to develop a Mediterranean garden. Your needs and desires will vary.

...a walk in your garden can be a sensual feast...

Whatever your choice of theme, or combination of themes, make sure it will work in your particular location – if you are gardening on a roof or balcony steer clear of anything that depends on heavy construction and large or wind-sensitive plants; if your garden is cool and shady all attempts to grow sun-worshipping plants will bring you nothing but frustration.

If you have a hot garden and want to combine intensive salads and formal themes, you could grow salads in the slight shade of intricately trained espalier apples, pears or even peaches with herb underplanting; this would keep the roots of your fruit trees cool, stop your salads from wilting and provide the hot aspect necessary for your Mediterranean herbs. Whatever your design, follow the golden rule to a healthy and productive garden: always help plants to help themselves.

CONTAINER CANDIDATES

Whatever your space, you can use it, but there is little more disappointing than sowing your seeds in great anticipation, then waiting, and waiting, and waiting… in vain. Some plants are more difficult to grow than others, some will grow anywhere and you'll have a job to stop them. You can grow most vegetables happily in permanent raised beds, as long as the soil is good and there is some sun, but not everything is so easy in containers. This page offers a brief resumé for beginners which I hope will help tentative container gardeners to avoid disappointment. If a vegetable is not listed, try it, but good results are not guaranteed.

Easiest container vegetables

Potatoes; chard; lettuces; radishes; shallots; bush tomatoes; peppers; egg plants; courgettes and squash; dwarf carrots; dwarf beetroot; Oriental greens; runner beans. Salad greens need virtually no care once they are established. Most salads are easy, everyone can find space for a pot of tomatoes in summer, and peppers and egg plants will be happy on a sunny windowsill.

Difficult in containers

Cauliflower; cabbage; sprouts; kale; parsnips and all deep rooting vegetables; swedes and turnips; celeriac.

Good in light shade

Peas (grow dwarf varieties in containers); lettuce; spinach; radishes; leeks; garlic; rhubarb; Oriental greens; chard, perennial salad greens.

Sunworshippers

Sweetcorn; tomatoes; peppers and chiles; egg plants and okra. They will grow in a northern garden but crops are rarely large.

Hungry container candidates

Potatoes; tomatoes; leeks; zucchini and squash; sweetcorn, broad beans. All love rich soil.

T O O L S

You don't need much equipment to have a productive small garden. If you are growing in containers all you need is a good pair of gloves, a trowel, a small fork, a pair of secateurs and a small pruning saw, seedling modules, perhaps a small barrow, a penknife, and some light string for temporary ties. A watering can is most important of all.
It may be helpful also to have a spade, a dibber and a pricking out tool.
If you have one or two raised beds you need little more, except a full sized fork and a rake. A small push mower will be adequate for any small patches of grass.

It is best to have an outdoor space to store any pots that are not being used, plus a seed tray or two, and perhaps a bag of compost, as well as a small compost bin (*see pages 41-43*). You will probably be able to create a hidden storage space in the garden, for example under a seat. Most small scale gardeners keep a trowel and fork handy in the kitchen.

Always clean equipment before you put it away. This not only prolongs the life of your tools, it also prevents the potential spread of any diseases.

TIPS AND TECHNIQUES

Using space
Garlic matures over a long
season, in spring use the
space between plants in
containers or raised beds
for salads

Once you have decided exactly what you want to grow, and how, and designed a garden to suit the needs of your household, you will find that careful planting can greatly increase the productivity of even a few containers. If you understand a few simple growing principles this can help you to produce far more food than you might at first expect.

Catch-cropping

Plants grow at different rates, so take advantage of this to grow fast-growing plants between slower ones, even if you are growing exclusively in containers. The idea is to "catch" one crop before the other one matures. Radishes for example can be sown in early spring with leafy salads to produce a crop in as little as ten days between the other seedlings. Garlic can be planted in tubs in autumn, then the growing plants can be surrounded by faster growing lettuces or salad mixes in spring, cropping the salad from May onwards and the garlic from July. In deep containers you can sow baby carrots at the same time as parsnips, and the carrots will crop well before the parsnips' leaves touch.

Different root space

Slow-growing plants produce deeper root systems to allow for changes in temperature over the season, whereas fast-growing plants produce smaller roots nearer the surface to minimize the energy used in root production. In containers the best way of taking advantage of this is growing annual vegetables or herbs in sunny spaces under fruit trees but if you're growing in raised beds you could experiment more widely.

Watch intensively planted containers closely as they need heavy feeding and watering to maintain nutrient levels.

Cut-and-come-again

Have all the ingredients for a tasty, colorful salad or stir-fry growing in the same place by mixing a range of leaves within the same container, trough or bed, preferably near the backdoor. You can purchase packets of mixed salad leaves or mesclun, or grow salad-bowl lettuces, rocket, wild celery, and chives together in small patches for a range of annual and self-seeding salads. Oriental greens and spinach are a good growing combination for stir-fries, and you can allow some plants to mature for late season use. Try one of the mixtures sold under names such as Spicy Mix or Braising Mix which contain a range of leaves suitable when

...take account of your abilities and don't aim too high at the start ...

very young for salads as well as stir fries. You can cut them hard for several crops through the summer and resow at regular intervals for continuous supply as the seeds mature very quickly and are ready for eating within four weeks.

Both cut-and-come-again salads and Oriental vegetables provide attractive crops with leaves in a range of colors from palest green to deep red and shapes ranging from starkly geometric to softly ruffled. Perennial salad beds can provide tasty leaves very early in spring and can be cropped all year as well as providing a living mulch and weed suppressant for fruit trees in large containers.

Providing shade

Plants grown for late winter or spring foods often have to be started in hot weather the previous summer, but need cool weather to flourish. If you are growing in containers move plants such as sweet fennel and Chinese vegetables into the shade in summer and into the light in autumn, but in beds you can plant them in the shade of taller species such as beans and sweetcorn that are cropped in the autumn. Squash and other trailing or large leaved plants can provide cooling shade at the base of taller plants such as sweetcorn or tomatoes.

Underplanting
Perennials are planted under
this blueberry shrub as
groundcover and to attract
beneficial insects

Using plants as support

Save on canes! You could grow about three climbing bean plants up a strong stemmed fruit tree as long as the tree is more than five years old. Or try growing a tub of sweetcorn in heavily manured soil and using several of the stalks to support their own climbing bean. Beans are an excellent companion for corn, the corn providing support and the beans nitrogen to feed the soil.

Miniature Forest Garden

Help your plants to help themselves by growing plants with different habits in a sun facing wedge shape (emulating the growing levels at a forest's edge). This works well in a small border, or even a large container such as a half barrel: from the back of the bed to the sunny front plant the tallest fruit tree, then smaller fruiting shrubs, then medium sized herbs and vegetables, followed by groundcover strawberries and herbs, with root crops if you're growing them in a raised or permanent bed, and climbing beans that use the taller plants as support.

Filling the gaps

Keep a tray or two of seeds propagating on your windowsill or in trays outside all year round, then when you go out to crop a plant, take a little rich compost and a couple of seedlings with you, and use the space right away. Or fill spaces with thinnings from lettuces, chard or spinach, or drop in a few seeds – if you don't use that space, then a weed probably will. Use the compost to feed the soil, and to provide a weed-suppressing mulch around your plants.

ROTATION

If you have any raised permanent beds, you should try and practice some kind of rotation system of your annual vegetables to keep the soil in good condition and disease-free. Different types of plants require a different balance of nutrients to succeed, and if you grow the same annual plant in the same place year after year you may end up with an unbalanced soil, with increased probability of disease, and the certain knowledge that every pest of that plant will know where to eat! If you plant the same crop in the same place two or more years running you run the risk of establishing the perfect habitat for pests and diseases that live in the soil in the off-season, ready to attack as soon as their food crop reappears.

Changing the type of plant in succession will ensure that your soil will stay balanced throughout the season, and from year to year. If you feed the soil in your small garden regularly with compost it can stay fertile, but it is still a good plan to practice rotation to provide for the needs of different plants. Most rotation systems are based on legumes, brassicas, roots and onions. Legumes fix nitrogen from the air, brassicas need a lot of nitrogen for leafy growth, roots have a deeper root zone to draw deeper nutrients, and onions require low nitrogen levels in order to bulb up. So the classic growing order of beans, cabbages, carrots and onions, follows logically from the needs of the plants. When you rot down your vegetable waste, the compost will have the same balance of nutrients. Perennial plants have time to make deeper roots, so they can draw minerals from subsoil and base rocks. You can add the leaf fall from trees, and regular cuttings of comfrey and nettles to your compost to boost mineral levels.

With very small plots it is best to grow a combination of plants in the same place, so drawing on a balanced range of nutrients. When you are growing in small containers you need to replace the entire growing medium every time a crop finishes, and every two to three years in large ones, top-dressing with good quality compost and mulching annually as well as feeding regularly to maintain soil health.

M O V A B L E   F E A S T S

You shouldn't ever have a conflict between your growing space and your enjoyment of that space. The best thing about containers is their versatility, which is why they're perfect for small gardens. You can change the scene in your garden at will, even large containers don't have to be permanently sited but you can place them on a plywood base with castors attached to move them around. If you have tender trees such as figs that may need winter protection, you can wheel them into a protected site for the winter then replace them in the sun in spring. If you have some containered fruit trees that lack sun early in the season, move them into the sun. A salad pyramid, made of a strong triangular frame of poles on a mobile plywood disc, with numerous 20cm (8in) pots hooked on, can be moved into the sun early in the season and out of the sun on hot days. Or if you just fancy a change, or want to sit and entertain you could just wheel your pots to one side for a while.

A mobile mint and strawberry tower
Upturn an old plastic bin on a compost filled car tire fixed to a circle of plywood fitted with 4 castors. Cut 6cm (2in) holes, 25cm (10in) apart all over the sides of the bin, and cut off the top (the old bottom). Carefully plant strawberry plants through the holes from the inside up, filling up with a rich compost between the plants.
It is a good idea to spiral a length of porous soaker hose up inside as you go. Then place a basin that can be filled with water on top of the tower, fit a hose attachment and connect it to the soaker hose. Place a smaller pot planted with mints standing on a brick inside the tower. When you fill the large basin with water, strawberries and mints can be watered simultaneously.

You can create quite large mobile structures with plants at different levels and on all sides. Always place the mass low down, and make sure that wind can be diffused through any structure which needs to be sturdy enough to withstand turbulent weather. But anything that needs to be moved about also needs to be reasonably light. Use plastic containers, and several stacked tires on a plywood base make a useful large mobile planter, which can be painted to look more attractive.

Mobile plantings are an excellent way to get to know what your plants like and what your garden can provide in terms of aspect and microclimate. In a small container-based garden, having your containers on wheels can allow you to change the shape of your plantings dramatically very quickly, for different weather conditions, or to make room when guests arrive.

STRUCTURES

Pergolas, arches, bowers and obelisks are very versatile garden structures, capable of adding a touch of formality or whimsy to even the smallest gardens. You can construct your own, as simple or fancy as you like, or buy one from a garden center or mail-order catalog, but make sure that any free-standing structure adds to the productivity of your site rather than throwing your best vegetables into shade.

Wherever you travel in the southern Mediterranean you come across pergolas covered in vines, shady and productive areas for sitting or working under. You can use this idea in any sunny space, training fruit trees to form an arch, or training climbing fruits over an arch or pergola to make a shady bower or to mask working spaces in the garden. In a small garden a tree-training arch will be able to support climbing annuals as well as fruiting trees. You can make an arch, supporting beans and squashes, in front of a sunny kitchen window to provide summer shade; fruiting

arches or canopies give a feeling of a larger garden around the edge of a balcony, or use a tree arch to demarcate areas of a roof garden. An obelisk makes a striking centerpiece to a bed of lower growing plants, or an attractive and useful feature to support climbers in a large container.

If you're constructing your own pergola, use substantial 7.5cm (3in) square-section or stripped-pole timber verticals, perhaps held apart with trellis at the side, and fix the main frame to some short posts in the ground rather than sinking long verticals which will inevitably rot in time. Make your pergola at the polar end of your garden, at an entrance, so that it throws the least shade on productive beds.

Making a tree-training arch

A tree-training arch must be constructed in winter as you should plant bare-rooted fruit trees. The arch should be raised on at least four posts at least 1m (3ft) apart. Embed 65cm (26in) long by 5x5cm (2x2in) posts at least 45cm (18in) deep in the ground. Place a flat stone or tile beside each post for the main arches to sit on, to help stop wooden posts from rotting. Fix a joined double lightweight arch made from metal, or bent and tied hazel poles or bamboo to the short posts, and plant four fruit trees on semi-dwarfing rootstocks.

Choose trees carefully: if you are having a mixed fruit arch, make sure each is self-pollinating, and they need to grow at roughly the same speed. Train the trees to the poles, and keep them pruned as single stem cordons. When the tops of the trees meet, you can cut off the growing tips, or graft them together.

Custom-made structures
In an urban setting metal arches and towers of scaffolding poles look entirely appropriate, and provide added vertical growing space as well as visual interest

PRUNING & TRAINING

Unless you intend to have an entirely wild garden, or grow nothing but salads in containers, you will need to prune a plant at some time. This encourages better yields, easier cropping, and continued health. You need to learn when to prune, but this is less frightening than it sounds and most plants will eventually recover from being pruned at the wrong time. Tool maintenance is most important: keep saws, knives, and secateurs sharp, and clean them regularly with a little methylated spirit before each use.

Restorative pruning

When you take on a garden you may inherit some trees, bushes and shrubs that you want to keep but they might be over large, or neglected and unproductive. Old fruit trees are classic items for restoration. If you feel uncertain about tackling a large pruning job yourself it is better to employ a professional rather than doing a poor job yourself, but if you have the confidence, you'll find it is not difficult to prune an old unproductive and straggly tree into something productive and attractive.

The first task in restoring an old fruit tree is to cut out any deadwood, next remove any crossing branches, and finally

...keep pruning tools sharp and clean...

prune to a productive shape. Be brave, it is better to make a few large cuts than lots of little ones. On a very large apple tree it is possible to cut back so that only the trunk and three main branches survive – stored energy in the root system lets the tree produce a mass of new growth that will form the basis for new training. If you have a substantial tree that needs to be cropped via a ladder you need to leave five or six main branches for support, with nearly all fruiting spurs within easy reach, like a large flat bowl. In most small gardens you will probably crop all trees from the ground, so prune to a pyramid shape, leaving the centre of the tree as clear as possible, pruning so that only outward-facing spurs and branches will grow.

Sawcuts should always be made from the underside of branches to ensure a clean break with no torn bark. Also slant your cuts to make sure that rain runs off easily. It is best to leave the cut area free to heal naturally, although some trees such as peach and dwarf stone fruit are more prone to disease, so use a proprietary wound paint on large cuts, leaving smaller ones (made with secateurs) to heal naturally.

When to prune

Prune apples, pears, gooseberries, and currants when they are dormant in winter. Prune stone fruit (cherries, plums, gages, damsons, peaches, etc) in late spring. Prune summer raspberries, brambles, and hybrid berries straight after harvest, cutting back all the branches that have just fruited, and tying the following year's branches to the supports as most woody fruiting plants produce best fruit on one year-old wood.

Most perennial herbs benefit from a light pruning in spring to remove dead wood, and a hard pruning just after flowering in late summer. This ensures a continuous supply of fleshy leaves for the kitchen and keeps plants compact. Most herbs need to be replaced every few years, and pruning is a good way of generating a supply of cuttings, which can be rooted, potted, then planted out in different places to replace old stock.

Pruning annuals

Prune annuals to encourage repeat cropping – cut-and-come-again is a pruning regime. Tall supported tomatoes (as opposed to bush or trailing varieties) will need to have lateral branches removed so that they can be trained vertically.

Trained pear

Fruit trees were often trained in
large grand gardens in Britain
in the 19th century, as well as to
conserve space, and many old
apple and pear trees of well
over 100 years old can be found
in the walled gardens of
Victorian country houses

Training

One feature which really sets apart a small plot from a large one is the need to train plants to unnatural shapes to maximize growing volumes. It is almost impossible to grow reasonable amounts of tree fruit in a small garden without training trees into compact, often flat, shapes. Flat trained trees are easy to pick, take little space, and the fruit is given an even solar aspect. Other decorative shapes can make powerful statements, and a fruit arch can make an excellent transition between productive spaces, or along a sunny passageway, providing shade and fruit. Whatever the size and design of your plot, there is always room for a container or two of trained fruit.

...training helps trees to produce heavily...

The main choices for the edges of small gardens are fan trained fruit, cordons and espaliers. There are also a number of shapes specially developed for tiny gardens and many nurseries offer a number of dwarf trees suitable for growing in containers, some that resemble miniature standards and others that crop very heavily on spurs only a short distance away from the central trunk. Step-over fruit are trained with lateral branches no more than 50cm (18in) from the ground so that you can grow fruit right at the front edge of a vegetable or herb bed. With normal annual maintenance pruning, trained trees will put more energy into producing fruit.

You can buy ready-trained fruit trees in a small range of varieties, but if you want specific varieties you will have to train them yourself, choosing trees grafted onto dwarfing or semi-dwarfing rootstock. Training is not difficult: tie bamboo canes to a tensioned wire frame and train the trees to the canes, using adjustable ties and replacing them annually. New growth on trees is quite flexible and it is fairly straightforward to bend the spurs gently on to their training frame, pruning off any that are irrelevant to the design. It usually takes a minimum of three years to build the main structure of a fan, espalier, or arch.

On single-sided designs all branches that grow towards the wall or fence should be cut off completely, while branches that grow outwards, or above and below a main stem, are cut to the first bud to produce fruiting spurs. The procedure differs slightly between species, so ask your nursery for initial advice when you purchase your tree, and refer to a comprehensive pruning guide (see Bibliography p.156).

NEW WAYS WITH WALLS

Anyone who has seen the delightful floral walls in the narrow whitewashed streets of Andalucia cannot ignore the growing potential of walls, and the inventiveness of the gardeners with the techniques they use to water their hanging gardens. Most are watered from upper windows, some use hose sprays, some have containers that are lowered on ropes, some gardeners use home-made irrigation systems, while others climb ladders with watering cans. When you design vertical gardens to make the most of wall space, you have to give some thought to watering methods, as well as to suitable plants.

The easiest way to make a wall into a productive space is to grow edible climbers up a trellis, which should be fixed at least 5cm (2in) away from the wall. This not only gives the plants room to thread their way upwards without endless tying in of branches and stems, it also allows small birds (which eat insects and molluscs) to nest in boxes provided for them. It is also more straightforward watering ground-level plants rather than wall-mounted containers.

If you are growing large perennial climbers such as blackberries, loganberries or kiwi fruit in permanent beds, you should plant them at least 30-45cm (12-18in) away from the base of the wall to avoid foundation damage and root constriction. Figs in containers should also be placed about the same distance from the wall to give sufficient room for the branches to grow. Large climbers may even act like an outer skin to keep a building a comfortable temperature throughout the growing season.

Wall boxes

Any sunny wall can be used to support a series of wall boxes, at every level. You can attach growing containers to the wall itself, using all kinds of expanding plugs and bolts, but it is safest and most flexible to fix a frame to the wall. This means that vertical loads are

Fruit for sunny walls
fig, kiwi fruit, fan-trained peach, fan-trained sweet cherry, fan-trained greengage

Vegetables for sunny walls
trailing marrows, squashes and pumpkins, mangetout peas, climbing French beans, tall tomatoes, cucumbers

Fruit for cooler walls
blackberry, loganberry, tayberry, fan-trained sour/Morello cherry, fan-trained late-flowering apple

Vegetables for cooler walls
runner beans

transmitted to the ground via the frame, rather than imposing pulling loads on the wall bolts. A structure using scaffold poles is ideal as it allows you to arrange a pulley system for raising and lowering containers, and provides a structure to hide any watering system you may devise. Lower, smaller wall boxes could be fixed on trellis, either above or between climbing plants.

The more functions every structure in your garden can perform, the more productive your garden will be. For example, peach trees in many areas are susceptible to peach leaf curl, a disease that is transmitted by rain, so a line of containers mounted above a fan-trained peach could provide some protection and possible support for a protective winter screen.

Rampant climbers
Squash have rampaged over
the wall and are escaping
along the pavement outside
this suburban garden in
Luxembourg

PATIO

Even if your house doesn't have much of a garden it may have a patio or yard. This might be little more than a small paved area adjacent to the house, or it could be a substantial hard standing area. Most patios are primarily used as an outdoor extension of the house, and can be a perfect place to grow a surprisingly large amount of produce simply by adding a few containers of varying sizes with perhaps a windowbox along with some permanent plantings of herbs and possibly a fruit tree. Add a few upright supports for climbers to provide an edible canopy over a table and chairs, plant your walls where possible, and you could have a thoroughly productive area which is also attractive and perfect for relaxing in. Movable containers can come into their own on small patios too (*see p.83*).

Patios are usually positioned to make the most of the sun, but are often partially shaded by adjacent buildings. On the plus side, adjacent buildings also provide shelter so you are unlikely to suffer too harshly from frosts, and the growing season will be longer than in a more exposed plot. If the patio faces the sun, the garden may be a whole climate zone warmer than less sheltered gardens in the same area. However, with a polar-facing garden the reverse can be true. While radiant heat from other buildings can help the lack of direct sunlight, such a situation can severely limit the growing of sun-ripened fruit or vegetables, so you should add as much light as possible to northfacing patios by painting walls or placing mirrors in strategic places.

Many patios, being so close to the house, hide all the utility pipes and drains and mains services under the paving or hard landscaping. So think carefully before you dig anything up! You can't plant even a small fruit tree in the ground if its roots are going to grow into sewerage or water pipes, or interfere with your electricity supply cables or earth wires, and it can be embarrassing and expensive, time-consuming and potentially even dangerous to attack the ground with a pickaxe only to find you've hit drains or a mains supply. So find out what's under there before you start.

Patio planting
Start your growing adventure
with a few pots of herbs and
edible flowers on a sunny patio

If your patio is paved you may be able selectively to lift the pavers for planting, or lift a section to build a raised bed or to plant climbers against a wall or to cover a pergola or arch. But containers offer great versatility and a lack of permanence that suits many gardeners. And some containers can make striking focal points even when there is nothing growing in them.

Containers allow you to start small, and add to your patio garden as you get more confident. Once you realize the joy of growing a few herbs, for example, you could perhaps add some edible flowers such as marigolds or a rose bush or honeysuckle, perhaps some soft fruit such as a tub of raspberries or a pot full of strawberries, and a container grown fruit tree – lots of nurseries now supply varieties with habits to suit container growing.

To make the most of your patio's growing potential, assess how much room you want for entertaining or just being outside, and use the rest of the space for a mixture of pots, permanent planters, troughs and raised beds if you can get to the soil. If you make the edging of the raised beds sturdy enough you can use them as extra seating and to support small and lightweight pots. You may be able to divide a sitting area from the rest of the patio with a trellis screen that you can use to support climbers, or construct a small pergola or arbor over the table area. It may be possible to cover much of your wall space with trellising, and different level troughs. A tiled sowing and potting area could double as a work surface for the barbecue. You may even have room for a mini greenhouse or hot box. If your patio is close to the kitchen, then a worm bin is a useful addition, as is a rain barrel if a roof downpipe runs nearby.

Many seed companies provide special ranges of "patio vegetables" designed for heavy cropping in small spaces, but grow a few large plants for more drama in a small space. And limited space doesn't mean you have to give up traditional vegetables. Although it probably won't be worth growing brassicas on a patio – they take months to mature, pests adore them and they can get a bit smelly, there are plenty of suitable fast-growing leafy salads, spinach and chards. Interplant with chives, spring onions, and garlic. Use any spare (fresh) garlic bulbs for planting and cut the leaves for salads – they rarely make very large mature bulbs when grown in tight spaces. Tomatoes are always worth growing in any sunny spot as they will have much more flavor than any you can find in the shops. Choose the small tumbling cherry types to begin with, along with a couple of thin-skinned salad ones. High value salad ingredients such as Oriental greens, colored lettuces and arugula grow easily in containers, and if you have a large container or raised bed make room for mangetout peas (on twiggy supports), French beans and perhaps a squash.

Make your patio work for you, concentrate on growing fresh leaves that don't keep well, aromatic herbs, and perhaps a favored fruit that would benefit from close attention. Most importantly, experiment and have fun.

S M A L L   B A C K   G A R D E N

Many small suburban and even urban back gardens can be used to grow a vast amount of food, and careful planning can mean that there is also enough space for entertainment and other garden uses. I have been almost self-sufficient in fruit and vegetables for eight years in my own small garden (*see pp. 148– 154*) which consists of three growing areas of 25 square meters (250 square feet). It shows what can be achieved in a small polar-facing space – of course there has been some experimentation, some successes and failures, but the secret of growing intensively in such a small space is good design.

The greatest advantage this kind of garden has is access to soil. Even if a back garden begins as nothing more than some grass seed thrown on to some leveled rubble, the potential benefits of being able to grow in soil outweigh disadvantages of having to

lay out permanent beds. Unless you have serious hard pan you can have a productive, fertile soil very quickly just by building raised beds directly on the grass. Hard pan is a concrete-like layer of subsoil, usually caused by compression of the soil by heavy machinery; if you want to make beds on hard pan you will have to break it up first with a pickaxe or pneumatic drill so the soil can drain and plants can mine the subsoil for nutrients.

I used railroad ties to contain and mark out raised beds which I made directly on the grass. Deep mulch beds (*see p.35*) are an excellent method of accelerating soil-building, buffering most nutrient deficiencies in your subsoil and excluding light to weeds. If you have the opportunity, do try to create beds as a living soil is the key to low maintenance and healthy plants. While containers are wonderfully flexible and can be used in almost any situation, if you try to add earthworms to improve the soil they will probably try to leave after the first heavy watering!

A rectangular back yard

With a rectangular garden it is best to plant fruit trees in the corners, then plant shrub fruits – currants, raspberries, blueberries – and woody herbs in front of the fruit trees. If you have the space, plant some ground cover, wild strawberries or a low growing perennial or self-seeding salad such as lamb's lettuce or arugula, if not make sure you mulch well.

...if you have the chance, build a few raised beds...

Train fruit trees around the perimeter (*see p.88*) or purchase those specially designed for tiny gardens, cropping heavily on tiny standard trees that reach no more than 1.5m (5ft) tall, spreading no more than 1m (3ft). The best way of choosing fruit varieties for permanent plantings in your garden is to check what local growers are growing successfully; many fruit varieties were originally developed to suit very specific areas, and those old varieties often thrive. However, balance this with the fact that modern varieties have usually been developed to crop more heavily, and in a small garden productivity will be a high priority. If your garden is subject to late spring frosts plant late-flowering varieties that will not be affected.

Just when you think you have no more space left around the edges plant climbers such as blackberries, loganberries, or tayberries to run along the top of fences or walls. If you have a warm garden it may be worth trying to train an outdoor grape.

Before you even look at the space left in the middle for raised beds and containers, a small back garden can accommodate over a dozen varieties of fruit, and a dozen herbs. Where the house throws shade in summer, and the aspect is a little dark to grow fruit successfully, make room for a decent sized hot-box: a compost box underneath with a coldframe on top to capture any heat produced by the composting process, a good place to start seedlings in spring. Other cooler areas can be used for rhubarb and mints, where a moist soil is important.

A warm fence space can be an ideal place for a small lean-to greenhouse for growing sun-loving plants and overwintering tender ones in cooler areas.

Once the edges have been attended to, lay out the central area. If you want to keep plenty of space for play or entertainment, grow in a series of containers with stepping stones or paths between. Use small containers in areas where you are more likely to want the space, arranging them around a larger (possibly wheeled) planter like an island. If you are most interested in maximizing your productive capacity then devote most of the area to raised beds. If you are careful in the design it is possible to have as much as 85% of the area productive, leaving only 15% for access, without having to walk on the soil,

...use every inch of fence and wall space, then fill the center...

though even this can be used to fit small movable pots or planters on wheels. This benefits the soil as walking on the soil compresses the soil structure and reduces its ability to supply plants with air and water, and saves the house from muddy footprints.

If you need paths, make them just wide enough to manouver a small wheelbarrow (*see p.62*) and edge the beds with material substantial enough to withstand the weather. While there are numerous options, depending on taste and resources (*see p.60*), I favor railroad ties as they are substantial, wide enough to place extra containers on top or to sit on, durable, inexpensive, and easy to work. For most people, a comfortable arm's reach is 60–70cm (2-2^1/$_2$ft), so make the beds double that width if you have access from both sides. It is also worth arranging the beds so that you have four or five equal sized areas, to allow easy vegetable rotation (*see p.82*).

In raised beds you can grow almost anything. Even deep-rooting parsnips and greedy plants such as celeriac are possible, patches of sweetcorn and even asparagus. The larger the growing area, the more flexible its use, particularly regarding efficient inter-cropping and catch-cropping (*see p.80*). However, even if you have deep beds, choose a range of miniature vegetables to capitalize on their generally shorter growing season. Crop spinach, chard and beet leaves when they are young and crisp, or even eat the thinnings as well as taking main crops. One year we were able to gather from our small back garden 15kilos (35lbs) of potatoes, 4.5kilos (10lbs) of parsnips, 12 heads of corn, along with 12kilos (25lbs) of other salads, leafy greens, root vegetables, rhubarb, herbs and fruit.

WEEDS

Weeds are the wrong plants in the wrong place at the wrong time. Most are pioneer wild plants. Every time you turn the soil you will bring weed seeds to the surface, where they will germinate. The seeds of most grasses, and many other wild plants (such as dandelions, thistles, teasels) are transported by wind, so even if you never till your soil you will get weeds.

In urban situations, where many more people grow exotic plants, the range of weeds that might pop up in your garden can be very wide. Some weeds may be self-sown from your own stock. Many herbs and perennial salad greens will self-seed easily, but they can be pulled up easily – and eaten!

Once you have a weed problem there are a number of ways of dealing with it. With edibles that spread by root division, such as mint and horseradish it is best to remove some good pieces of root for growing in a container, and kill the rest with a light-excluding mulch. Non-edible seedlings can be killed by hoeing or through continuous mulching, but vigorous culprits such as dandelions and thistles need a great deal of hoeing or mulching as they have a sizeable store of energy.

The most difficult weeds to deal with are root-propagating plants that are part of larger networks. Quack grass is one common foe but do not start to dig the roots up unless you have huge resources of time and energy. Even the tiniest piece of root can become a new plant. However, the best way to deal with them is to try and eradicate them before you start growing anything in the garden, even if you are growing exclusively in containers.

If you do have the offending root-propagating plants on your patch, cut them down close to the ground. Then, although it may not look very beautiful, the surest way to get rid of them is to cover your plot for the first year in heavy layers of well-overlapped cardboard, hessian-backed carpet, or heavy black plastic, you will scarcely have a problem. When you remove it, pave or build raised beds on top. If you avoid digging your soil and make mulching part of normal garden maintenance, your weed problems will be few.

PESTS & DISEASES

There are many simple, non-poisonous ways of getting rid of pests from the garden, but wherever possible, prevention is better than cure. This can take many forms – putting up barriers, removing attractants, discouraging species that protect pests and encouraging creatures that eat them.

In general, place physical barriers such as horticultural fleece over young brassicas to protect them from flea beetles and harmful caterpillars. Use grease bands round tree trunks to protect trees from ants and codling moth larvae. Maintain flowering companions (such as chives) around fruit as aphid predators – adult hoverflies, lacewings, wasps, and ladybirds need nectar and will build up their populations of predatory larvae among the aphids. If aphid infestations get out of hand, then (non-biological) soapy water sprayed on the affected plants will make it difficult for them to cling on. Blackfly often appear on nasturtiums and broad beans so pinch out the tops as soon as the beans start to pod at the bottom.

Slugs and snails are lethal to salads and other green leaves, and no control method is foolproof. You can vigilantly manually pick off slugs on damp mid-spring evenings so there will be fewer of the tiny invisible ones that do most of the damage, or use saucers filled with beer as traps, but best of all, provide opportunities for natural predators. Frogs, beetles, and birds can be attracted into the garden with small sheltered ponds, piles of deadwood, and birdbaths. Birds are generally welcome in a garden (to control insect populations), but net fruits.

Fungal and bacterial diseases take many forms. The bacterial and fungal spores are present almost everywhere in the air, looking for an opportunity to settle and multiply. Avoid disease with good garden hygiene, a healthy soil and a good watering regime. Most fruit cankers are the result of wounds not healing properly, so always clean your pruning tools with methylated spirit before and after use.

Attractive pests
Some pests, such as tomato hornworms found widely in the United States, may not look unpleasant – but they will happily decimate your crop nonetheless

GOOD COMPANIONS

A good deal of mythology has built up over the years about companion planting, much of it identified with old farmers' and old wives' tales. It is true that much that passes as companion planting is simply the application of common sense, but this is now backed up by a substantial body of empirical and scientific evidence supporting the positive effects of planting certain species alongside specific companions (*see list on page 150*).

No amount of tinkering with companion plants will make up for poor soil, inappropriate microclimate, poor maintenance, or poor plant rotation. But if you start with the right soil conditions and solar aspect for your plants, companion combinations will help you to maintain healthy and productive plants. Companion gardening is not a substitute for poor planting and planning, it is more like the icing on a very rich cake.

If you grow plants of the same family closely together this is bound to put a strain on available resources, and make it more likely that all plants will get the same disease, or attract the same pest. On the other hand, if you plant legumes with heavy feeders this brings together nitrogen fixers and nitrogen users in the same spot, and planting species with different root zones close together uses nutrients at different levels. Or bring together plants that attract pest predators with plants that are attractive to pests. Flowering herbs and flowers among fruit and vegetables will attract mature lacewings, hoverflies, and ladybirds; the adults will then lay eggs or produce larvae amongst a nearby aphid population, which will use them as food until they become adults.

Some plants are also said to control pests, weeds or plant disease by means of chemicals in the roots or scent; the roots of Marigolds (*Tagetes*) for example, produce a nematode-repelling chemical. Tomatoes excrete certain enzymes from their roots which discourages weeds such as quack grass.

One of the biggest questions when using companion plants is how close, and how many. A general rule of thumb for legumes and nitrogen feeders is to plant one to one, each within 20cm (8in) of each other. When planting for pest predators, it is usually

adequate to have some small flowers within 50-75cm (2-3ft) of the pest attractor, but it is probably best to place containers of herbs alongside pots of vegetables, or edge vegetable beds with flowering herbs. To use the scent or root chemicals of a plant, then the closer the better; use at least one companion to three food plants, though equal numbers would be better. But no companion will make up for a poor growing situation, and make sure there is enough room for all the plants to grow, or your companion plants will end up reducing your yields!

Supporting role
Marigolds are excellent
companions for most fruit
and vegetables, here they
help repel pests from a
container-grown squash

B A L C O N I E S

Balconies vary greatly in overall size, aspect and altitude, and in construction and load-bearing capacity. If your space is very high off the ground or on the edge of a building, then you are likely to be buffeted by wind, making the growing of delicate annuals only possible with some protection. In addition your balcony may be your only outdoor space, or may be merely an addendum to an upstairs room. The design and layout of your balcony garden will be dependent on a whole number of factors.

...before you start, always check what weight your balcony will take...

Watching your weight

Generally balconies are designed to support loads equivalent to a balcony full of people but you must check the load bearing capacity before you start any major project – for example you may want to entertain a balcony load of people and additional garden weight might be dangerous. Check with a civil engineer before you add to or alter your balcony.

Any balcony that is cantilevered from the building on only one side is not likely to be very strong, and you will need to use the wall for supporting heavier structures. Soil and water are heavy, so place any large containers close to a structural wall, not near the front edge or center of an unsupported balcony. If supported on two or more sides then you can place large growing boxes around the perimeter. Always use lightweight soil or compost in high rise gardens.

Using the aspect

Ground-level gardeners can often compensate for a less-than-ideal aspect with clever planting, shading and use of light and reflective materials, but aspect can be more of a problem on balconies as they tend to either concentrate heat or shade most of the day.

North-facing balconies generally only get direct sun for a few hours in high summer, so suit fast-growing annuals during the summer, with perhaps some hardier climbing fruit such as blackberries or loganberries for a perennial dimension. A large sun-facing balcony can support a wide range of food plants year round, with added heat from the building's walls used to transfer heat to tender plants in trellis against the walls. If nights are very cold you can use the the day's heat stored in the walls to protect trellis-trained plants by draping horticultural fleece, blankets or insulated aluminum foil over them.

If your balcony is shaded overhead, growing plants with a high light requirement may be difficult, though the overhead shade can be protective in hot summer sun, while allowing low winter sun to penetrate for winter salads.

Wind is often a serious problem in high level balcony or roof gardens. The relatively small gaps between buildings tend to concentrate winds which can be highly turbulent and could easily break or stunt the growth of any open grown tree, or destroy a flimsy trellis. You will need to deflect or diffuse wind by erecting flexible fencing up to 2.4m (7ft) high around a balcony or roof space, which can be left bare or used to support climbers such as runner beans, kiwi fruit, or fan trained plums against. You could use sturdy trellis, slats of wood or bamboo, or any rigid pierced material, as long as it is firmly attached to the perimeter.

The relationship between your balcony and any other possible growing spaces must also be taken into account. If you have a large garden outside and your balcony is outside a bedroom, then the balcony is best used for views over the garden, with perhaps a few strawberries and fragrant herbs and flowers outside to tempt you on sunny mornings. However, if the balcony is your sole outdoor space then it becomes far more important to use the space efficiently and productively.

Standard practice

A number of techniques are relevant to any balcony design. When there is no overhead shade, use high level growing boxes, supported on scaffold poles that transfer vertical loads to load-bearing supporting walls. Deep lower boxes can support very-dwarfing fruit trees trained to the walls and surrounded by herbs and shallow-rooting salads, and if boxes are large enough they could even support a fruiting shrub or two such as blackcurrants or blueberries. Troughs along the edge of a balcony become very exposed in winter and should be used for annual vegetables such as spinach, dwarf beans and courgettes, possibly using alkathene or bamboo hoops in the troughs to support annual climbers. High level troughs could be used for ground-level or trailing fruit and vegetables such as tumbling tomatoes and strawberries as well as short-lived annuals.

Start seeds and cosset seedlings on windowsills or in front of a glass balcony door, and remember to find a convenient space to store hand tools, a watering can and a small compost container or a worm-bin. If there is the space, fit a small rainwater tank in the corner (where the balcony is strongest) which can be fed from the adjacent down-pipe *(see pp.49)*. When your productive zone is so close to your living space it is very easy to keep an eye on things for problems or readiness for the kitchen. The sowing and potting area is adjacent to the seedlings, tools and compost. Planting out can be as easy as turning around, cropping just a lazy reach.

Leave the center of your balcony clear enough for a small table and a few small pots – imagine the pleasure of reaching down to pick strawberries for breakfast, or picking a sprig of rosemary to flavour a high-rise barbecue. It is always a good idea to maintain some year-round herbs and perennial spaces so that predator insects can overwinter in comfort and so help you in pest control in the following year, although insect pests are unlikely to be a problem on a windy balcony which will suffer from different problems of wind drying, and possible breakage. High altitude gardens are probably best for the growing of very hardy fruits and herbs, with high-maintenance annuals for a few short summer months.

R O O F   G A R D E N S

City living
A perimeter mounted trough of
vegetables perches high above
New York city streets

More and more urban dwellers today are realizing the potential of roof gardens, but they are scarcely a new phenomenon. In 600BC Nebuchadnezzar II created the legendary Hanging Gardens of Babylon as a consolation to his Medean wife who missed the natural surroundings of her homeland. These were roof gardens, balconies and terraces overflowing with herbs, fruit and medicinal trees, as well as flowers.

First principles

The very first step, before you consider any roof garden design, is to seek professional advice from a structural engineer. Most flat roofs are designed to be accessed, and to take a certain locally assessed snow load, which is usually enough to take lightweight containers and planting, but always check carefully before you start. You can only go ahead when you have verified that your roof is structurally strong enough to support a garden, however humble your plans. You also need to make sure of good water drainage and ensure that you have or can create reasonable access to a water supply.

Roof gardens always have plenty of light, and uninterrupted weather, whether sun, rain, wind or snow, so your considerations will be quite different from those of earthbound gardeners. And you will have to overcome the exposure of your garden to extremes of weather, in hot climates roof gardens become baking sunspaces and require summer shading, in more temperate climates they can be windswept and cold.

Access can be a problem, but determined gardeners will find a way of hoisting materials onto a roof even if it means using a block and tackle to lift everything up from ground level. Where access is a problem, it is all the more important to make best use of materials, so recycle compost and compost all your waste (*see p.38-42*). The altitude doesn't only affect accessibility, it also has an enormous bearing on the design: the higher the space, the greater chance of wind damage, the most serious problem for many roof gardeners. A low-rise roof in a high-rise area may also

suffer from too much shade and extremes of wind, from stagnant summers to extremely turbulent winters. Very little edible will thrive in such conditions, except for the very hardiest perennial herbs.

The walls around a roof garden are likely to be the strongest structures because they have to resist outward buckling due to vertical loads. You may be able to use this strength not only to support troughs or decking but also for cantilevering troughs off the tops of the walls. Most domestic roofs will support substantial plants such as a tree in a large container fixed where the walls meet at the corners.

Find out where the rafters are so you know the safest positions to place large planters anywhere away from the edges of the roof, and use a free-draining lightweight compost to minimize weight increase after heavy rain. Many roof gardeners lay timber decking underfoot on roof gardens, this disguises ugly and uneven surfaces, helps with drainage, and assists in spreading the load of containers and installations.

High rise challenges

As with balcony gardening, the main challenge is likely to be wind, so you will probably need to diffuse it by erecting some sort of windbreak such as trellis or mesh or any kind of wall pierced with holes to dissipate the wind. Then you can create satisfactory growing conditions for almost anything, and there are many examples of roof orchards where the structural wall surrounding

...surround yourself with lush edible planting in the middle of a city...

a roof garden supports a cordon of fruit trees at least 2m (6ft) high trained to wires or strong trellis. The trees need to grow in lightweight troughs allowing for at least 50cm (20in) soil depth, with posts fixed to the wall to support the wire fencing. If you don't want to grow fruit trees against it, you could leave your wind barrier as a decorative protective screen, or grow sturdy climbers.

Glossy leaved bay trees are often grown in exposed situations, but you will have to move them off the roof or wrap them carefully for the winter as they need protection from all but the mildest frosts. Any plants growing in the exposed situation of a winter roof garden will need more protection than if they were growing at ground level.

An effective way of growing salads on a roof garden is to construct one or two raised troughs across the roof about 30cm (12in) deep, and no more than 90cm (3ft) wide for easy maintenance.

Place a small composter or worm bin close to where you access the roof, perhaps with a

small potting station on top of the lid with a small cupboard for pots and tools next to it. If you have the room it is certainly worth finding room for a hot box or small greenhouse somewhere in your design, somewhere to move your frost-sensitive plants in winter, and start your seedlings in spring. A preserved softwood frame with polycarbonate glazing is ideal – polycarbonate is a good material for roof gardeners, it is light, shatterproof and a good insulator – some people even use pierced polycarbonate panels as screens or windbreaks.

Hot box
Place rooftop seedlings in a glazed box to give them a protected early start

Access to a convenient water supply is one of the biggest problems for roof gardeners, particularly as plants dry out more on a roof than at ground level as they will be planted in shallow soil, and because of the wind factor. You may be able to instal wall-mounted perimeter tanks and catch some rainwater that way (*see p.49*). If you like solving problems through do-it-yourself, the difficulty of getting a water supply to the roof could even be sorted out by using the roof garden's greatest problem: wind. You could fix a small wind pump to the roof to raise water from a ground level rain tank. Or you may be able to plumb a standing pipe and faucet onto your roof.

If you can solve the main challenges of roof gardening – wind, extremes of weather, water, weight and access – you can treat your garden pretty much as any other. The increased shade-free exposure will mean greater wind drying, structural limitations mean greater attention to design, and the relative inaccessibility means greater effort in setting up. But any roof garden can provide with you with a private edible haven to attract birds and insects, and every roof that is planted brings a building to life. To be surrounded by lush edible planting in the middle of a city is a fine reward for the extra effort that it may take to get a roof garden established.

W I N D O W S I L L S

You don't need a garden at all to grow some food. Many people first experience the delights of picking fresh produce from the kitchen windowsill. It is an obvious place to grow herbs for the kitchen, and can be used for much more. Depending on the warmth of your kitchen, and its general humidity (most herbs prefer dry air, otherwise they show signs of mildew) you can grow windowsill herbs most of the year, though a high latitude, and a sunless kitchen window may limit winter light levels.

Pots on sills

A few pots of parsley, basil and coriander bring life to the kitchen and to the palate. You can buy pots of these and many other herbs from food stores, but those you grow yourself will last much longer – and cost a fraction of the price. They are easily started off in 8-10cm (3-4inch) pots filled with a light compost, just scatter the seeds sparingly on top and brush a little compost lightly over them. Cover pots with a transparent plastic bag to aid germination. If the nights are cool, and your window is not double glazed, then lift the pots off the windowsill and close the curtain. Once the plants develop and show more than four leaves you will need to keep an eye on them for water.

To avoid disappointment, choose your herbs carefully – the ubiquitous basil, for example, can be surprisingly difficult to grow; if you have difficulty getting a good crop of large leaved sweet basil going, try a small leaved variety such as Greek basil which seems less fussy about humidity and watering requirements. Also, small leaved basils grow into very satisfactory and longlived shrubby little bushes. Parsley requires more water and survives in less sun than coriander which requires more water than basil which prefers fairly arid and very light and warm conditions.

The kitchen window is also a good place to sprout seeds, like mustard and cress (on damp kitchen paper), or alfalfa, bean sprouts (mung beans) or chick peas in transparent containers. Wash seeds (apart from mustard and cress) in gently running water before placing them in a container, do this daily until the first leaves are about to appear, then start using them. It is best to do little and often to ensure a continuous supply.

Almost any windowsill in your home can be used for limited food production, especially those with a sunny aspect. Many people have house plants to cheer up rooms (these are usually sub-tropical plants suitable for low light levels), so there is no reason why some plants, placed close to windows, may not be edible. Ornamental chiles are a good example. They are easy to grow, enjoy warm dry conditions, and the pods can be used in the kitchen – some are very hot! Sunnier windowsills should be used for sun-demanding herbs and vegetables such as basil, tomatoes, peppers, chillies and egg plants, and the cooler windows could be for parsley, coriander and small round carrots, turnips and radishes. The performance of your windowsill will change through the seasons due to a change in sun angle and shade from other buildings.

Indoor troughs

Once you have mastered herbs in pots you could obtain some larger troughs and increase your indoor repertoire. You can successfully grow a few strawberry plants between herbs such as parsley, but beware of mildew, make sure that the room is well ventilated. Cut-and-come-again winter salad mixes sold as spicy mix or braising mix, containing mainly mustards and Oriental greens, have shallow roots and are unfussy about light and temperature so can thrive in windowsill boxes all year round. The key is always experimentation through the seasons, something that works well in one situation may fail completely in another.

If you have an outside garden, windowsills are an excellent place to start seeds and get seedlings growing well before planting them out. Tomatoes, peppers, sweetcorn and squashes need to be started on sunny windowsills as the light levels are crucial to the seedlings. Polar-facing windowsills are fine for cabbages, lettuce and other leafy plants. If you have tall windows you may consider making a shelf halfway up for more pots, or you could have a hanging basket dangling from the top for cherry tomatoes, shallow rooting salads or nasturtiums. Tall windows and

French doors or windows allow maximum light into a room so you may be able to grow sun-loving vegetables such as tomatoes, aubergines and peppers in containers or a trough at floor level inside the windows. Place them in a large plastic tray to stop water getting on the floor.

Outdoor sills

Windowboxes are excellent for gardeners with limited space. Relatively simple to construct and easy to maintain, they are suitable for all except high-rise apartment dwellers. In a low level apartment, no more three floors up, you may be able to cantilever a trough outside a sunny, sheltered window with a shallow sill so you can lean out comfortably. But always make sure you fix it securely, as a windowbox full of soil and plants is heavy.

A trough that extends 45-60cm (18-24in) on either side of the window could be used to grow climbers, trailers, or even a very dwarf tree – imagine reaching out of a third floor window to pick a peach for breakfast! A windowbox is ideal for quite substantial herbs such as rosemary, fennel or sage, for leafy vegetables and edible flowers such as geraniums and nasturtiums. Ground floor windowboxes could be surrounded with trellising or a lightweight arch to support climbing beans, trailing marrows or cucumbers.

Before you instal a windowbox make sure that the wall or windowframe can take the weight of the box, planting and soil. If you have a load-bearing masonry wall then you can fix a supporting galvanized steel frame to the wall using heavy-duty masonry fixings. A wood frame would be lighter, but may not last very long. Any frame should fit a large trough – recycled plastic is the first choice as it is light and fairly durable, but this will depend on the structure of your building, and how much you want to plant. If you do want to use a wooden trough, or a decorative terracotta one, remember the weight factor. If your building is wooden you will have fix a frame according to where the main building frame or studs occur, spreading the weight over as long

...make sure a windowbox is secured firmly in place...

a vertical distance as possible. If you have clapboarding you can't fix off the wall and can only fit a light box to the window frame.

External window boxes should be filled with a lightweight compost *(see page 38)*. Make sure that your container has drainage holes in the bottom, 20mm ($^3/_4$in) hole every 30cm (12in) is ideal; if you are confident that the structure is strong enough then you can drill a series of 10mm ($^1/_2$in) holes every 20cm (8in), 50mm (2in) from the bottom to make a small reservoir in a 30-45cm (12-18in) deep trough. Even if you have regular rain, you will have to check your windowbox daily to see that the compost is moist, as the trough may be in the building's rain shadow. In any case small seedlings will need gentle watering every day until their roots penetrate to the moister lower layers.

Once you have grasped the principles of growing food at your window, and experimented with different types and timings of planting at your different windows, you will be able to produce a significant amount of fresh, tasty food, even in winter. Remember that plants take longer to mature in winter, so concentrate on fast growing spinach and salads.

Chapter Three

WHAT SHALL I GROW?

Gather crisp or juicy vegetables, aromatic herbs, succulent fruit and subtle flowers…

VEGETABLES

Asparagus
Asparagus officinalis
Suitable for large tubs and raised beds
Size: Stems to 1.5m/9ft tall, 90cm/3ft wide and deep
This perennial vegetable is traditionally grown on large plots in a dedicated deep bed. Although one mature asparagus crown can grow as large as a man's head and shoulders, asparagus can be grown very successfully in a large container such as a discarded bathtub, filled with manure rich compost which is regularly revitalised with extra manure. Once established, asparagus requires virtually no maintenance, and flower stems and seed heads are very attractive so it is definitely a positive addition to a small plot.
Germination period: Buy crowns.
Sowing to harvest time: 2 years after planting 2 year old crowns.
Soil requirements: Humus-rich, free draining loam
Climate: Asparagus is a hardy perennial but dislikes very wet, cold climates.
Cultivation: In a deep tub or raised bed of rich loam in a sunny position plant crowns 20cm/8in deep, 45cm/18in apart in spring. Feed with a layer of manure annually. Crop in late spring from the 3rd year onwards..
Watch out for: Slugs, asparagus beetle.
In the kitchen: Delicious tender vegetable steamed, baked, roasted or grilled.
Varieties: Buy crowns from a specialist supplier.

Aubergines/Egg Plants
Solanum melongena
Excellent for Containers
Size: 60-90cm/2-3ft tall
Aubergines are excellent subjects for sunny windowsills or a conservatory, they need a long growing season to succeed outside.
Minimum container depth: 20cm/9in
Germination period: 10-20 days
Sowing to harvest time: 16-18 weeks
Soil Requirements: Rich well-drained compost.
Climate: Warm and humid conditions are best – ideally above 18°C/64°.
Cultivation: Sow in small pots on a sunny windowsill in spring, only put outside when the weather is quite warm. Liquid feed and feed with potash as the first fruits swell.
Watch out for: White fly and mildew.
In the kitchen: Stews & grilling.
Varieties: Moneymaker, Bonica, and look out for bushes bearing small white, purple or orange egg-shaped fruits which will yield well in containers but need more sun than the purple varieties.

Beet
Beta vulgaris
Good in containers and raised beds
Although beet can be round, oval or long rooted, and may be purple, golden or white, choose the small globe shaped varieties for containers as larger roots need deep containers.
Minimum container depth: 25 cm/10in
Germination period: 15-24 days
Sowing to harvest time: 8-12 weeks
Soil requirements: Light well-drained soil or compost
Climate: Beet need a cool climate, they are particularly good for Northern Europe.
Cultivation: Sow direct into the container or bed 5-10cm/2-4in apart, after the soil has warmed and frost passed by mid spring.Water well in dry conditions or the roots will become woody.
Watch out for: Birds.
In the kitchen: Salads, soup, side vegetable. Tops can be used for delicious steamed greens.
Varieties: Dwarf varieties such as Acton, Dwergina or Pronto are best in containers, or choose Snow White or the attractive red and white striped Barbietola di Chiogga for raised beds.

Beans – French/climbing beans
Phaseolus spp.
Attractive in large containers, most productive in raised beds
Size: 2-3m/6-10ft tall
French beans are fast-growing annuals which need a warm soil (over 12°C, 52°F) to germinate. Runner beans are less tender. In Northern Europe French and runner beans are usually grown for their immature green pods but elsewhere the shelled fresh beans or dried beans are popular. Not only good for the table, they are also attractive ornamental climbers with white, red or pink flowers from June onwards, and they fix and increase nitrogen in the soil.
Minimum container depth: 20cm/9 in
Germination period: 10-15 days
Sowing to harvest time: 12-14 weeks
Soil requirements: Neutral compost in containers; any fertile soil in raised beds
Climate: Beans grow across a wide climatic range, but they are generally tender. French beans and most of the varieties grown for drying flourish in hot dry conditions, while runner beans will not set seed if the temperature rises above 30°C/90°F.
Cultivation: Sow 2 seeds per pole 2.5cm/1in deep after the last frost. When a plant reaches the top of its

support pinch out the growing tip. For an early crop sow 2-4 seeds in 5cm/2in pots on the windowsill a month before the last frost, planting the strongest in a container or raised bed outside when at least four leaves are showing and frost danger is past. Keep beans well watered as flowers appear and in dry weather. Pick ripe beans regularly to encourage prolonged harvest.

Watch out for: Slugs on shoots, mice eating seeds, blackfly and greenfly.

In the kitchen: Use green beans fresh steamed, boiled, stirfried and in salads. Store dry beans and use them in soups, stews and cooked in salads.

Varieties: Select from smaller modern varieties for container growing but try old-fashioned climbing French beans such as Veitch's Climbing and Coco Bicolor if growing in raised beds. Czar is an attractive white flowered runner.

Beans – dwarf & bush beans
Suitable for containers and raised beds
Size: 30cm x 30cm/12in x 12in
Minimum container depth: 15cm/6in
Germination period: 10-14 days
Sowing to harvest time: 12 weeks
Soil requirements: Moisture-retentive non-acid soil
Climate: Frost tender, they need sun and shelter.
Cultivation: As for French/runner beans, but plant out 25-45cm/10-18in apart. You may need to support the bushes with twiggy sticks. Keep well watered and mulch in early summer. Harvest when pods are about 10cm/4in long.
Watch out for: Slugs on seedlings, mice on seeds, blackfly.
In the kitchen: Side vegetable, stir-fries. Can be dried as flageolet beans (when fully mature).
Varieties: Most dwarf bush varieties will grow happily in a container as long as they are kept well watered.

Broad Beans
Vicia faba
Not good in containers
Size: 40-100cm/15-40in tall
A useful early vegetable, grown for the fresh green beans, some varieties can be grown over the winter for an early spring crop. Broad beans sometimes need staking with twiggy sticks. Although you can grow broad beans in tubs, they are unlikely to crop well as they prefer space and a rich moist soil.
Minimum container depth: 20cm/8in
Germination period: 10-20 days
Sowing to harvest time: 3-4 months from spring sowing, 6-7 months from autumn sowing
Soil requirements: Fertile, moisture-retentive soil
Climate: Generally hardy, broad beans should not be over-wintered in areas with long cold winters.
Cultivation: Sow direct 15-25cm/6-10in apart in friable soil in October, protecting young seedlings from heavy frost with straw, or sow in early spring. When plants are in full flower pinch out the growing top to reduce scent attraction to blackfly. Harvest when pods are no more than 15cm/6in long for best flavour.
Watch out for: Slugs on seedlings, blackfly on tops.
In the kitchen: Side vegetable, soups, stews and stir-fries.
Varieties: The Sutton (compact for winter sowing), Bunyards Exhibition (for spring sowing).

Broccoli, Calabrese and Cauliflower
Brassica oleracea
Dwarf varieties in containers, otherwise raised beds
Size: up to 50cm/22in tall
Most brassicas take up space for a large part of the year, and are not really worth growing in very small spaces unless you are passionate about them, in which case, choose from the compact varieties that are appearing in many seed catalogues. Do not grow large varieties in pots, they take too long to mature, attract pests, and can become rather smelly!
Minimum container depth: 25cm/10in
Germination period: 7-12 days
Sowing to harvest time: from 17 weeks for dwarf varieties, otherwise 9-11 months
Soil requirements: Rich loam
Climate: Calabrese are frost tender, broccoli and cauliflower generally hardy.
Cultivation: Sow under cover all year round according to variety, then plant out traditional varieties in soil 45cm/18in apart with the lower leaves just above the surface, plant dwarf varieties 15cm/6in apart. Intercrop larger varieties on raised beds with dwarf beans or peas. Water plants well in dry conditions and feed container grown plants with liquid feed in mid-season. Brassicas like nitrogen-rich soil where beans have previously grown.
Watch out for: Flea beetles in spring and summer, club root if soil has little lime, caterpillars.
Varieties: Idol, King and Perfection cauliflowers have been developed specifically for patio growing.

Cabbage & Kale
Brassica oleracea
Dwarf varieties in containers, otherwise raised beds
Size: up to 50cm/22in tall
Forget about traditional tall varieties of kale and choose dwarf varieties, and if you have a passion for cabbages choose spring cropping varieties as the best value for

space: you can take a second crop off each cabbage plant by cutting the first head, then cutting a cross on the remaining stem which will then produce 4 smaller heads.
Minimum container depth: 20cm/8in
Germination period: 7-12 days
Sowing to harvest time: Depends on type and season of sowing
Soil requirements: Nitrogen-rich
Climate: Most varieties are very frost hardy. They need sun but don't like to get too hot.
Cultivation: As broccoli
Watch out for: Fleabeetle, slugs, cabbage root fly and Cabbage White butterfly.
In the kitchen: Coleslaw, side vegetable, savoury parcels, soups and stir-fries.
Varieties: Choose very compact varieties such as the spring cabbage Minicole, or Showbor dwarf kale.

Carrots
Daucus carota
Good in containers and raised beds
Traditional Amsterdam and Nantes types are ideal for finger size carrots, but carrots come in a wide range of colors, shapes and sizes, most suitable for container growing.
Minimum container depth: 20cm/8in
Germination period: 14-24 days
Sowing to harvest time: 10-18 weeks depending on variety
Soil requirements: Free draining sandy loam or compost. Carrots don't like rich heavy soil.
Climate: Hardy, carrots can be left in the earth over a mild winter as long as the ground does not freeze.
Cultivation: Sow direct 2-5cm/1-2in apart every 2-3 weeks in small patches from spring to late summer, thinning the plants when the foliage is about 5cm/2in tall. Firm the soil around carrots after thinning. Keep well watered.
Watch out for: Carrot fly – place a barier around the carrots 45cm/18in high, this could be a mesh, or simply tall plants. If soil is too rich carrots will have forked roots.
In the kitchen: Salads, soups, stirfries, cakes.
Varieties: Oxheart are short and stumpy, Jaune de Doubes are cylindrical, Parabel are spherical, or try miniature Gregory or Mignon for container growing.

Celery and Celeriac
Apium graveolens
Not good in containers, raised beds only
You can grow celery in a large container but it is not a sensible use of space, although it has striking foliage. Choose a self-blanching variety.
Minimum container depth: 30cm/12in

Germination period: 18-28 days
Sowing to harvest time: 14-26 weeks depending on variety
Soil requirements: Rich moisture-retentive loam or compost with high humus content
Climate: Suitable for most temperate climates but cold weather during early growth can make celery bolt.
Cultivation: Sow under cover for earlier cropping or straight into the earth in spring after danger of frost is passed. Plant seedlings 30cm/12in apart.
Watch out for: Slugs on seedlings.
In the kitchen: Salads, stews, soups.
Varieties: Golden Self Blanching celery, Snow White celeriac.

Chard / Leaf Beet
Beta vulgaris
Containers and raised beds
Size: 15-30cm x 60 cm/6-12in x 24in
Chard grows well in containers, and overwinters in all but the coldest areas. A very decorative vegetable, choose ruby red or rainbow colored varieties for maximum interest in containers.
Minimum container depth: 20cm/8in
Germination period: 10-20 days
Sowing to harvest time: 8-12 weeks
Soil requirements: Virtually any humus-laden soil
Climate: Chard thrives in cool northern climates, but can bolt if it gets too dry.
Cultivation: Sow in autumn or spring, thinning plants when they are about 10cm/4in tall (and eating the thinnings in salads). Plants crop almost all year round, pull outer leaves off and more will grow. You can even cut back to the crown in winter for an early crop in spring.
Watch out for: Slugs.
In the kitchen: Salads, steamed vegetable, stir fries, pasta dishes.
Varieties: Swiss chard, Rainbow chard, Ruby chard.

Courgettes / Zucchinis & Summer Squashes
Cucurbita spp.
Ideal for containers and raised beds
Size: Bush varieties 30-50cm x 50-75cm/12-20in x 20-30in; trailing varieties over 2m/6$^{1}/_{2}$ft long
There are hundreds of types of squashes, from small acorn shaped summer squashes and cylindrical courgettes or zucchinis to large round winter squash and pumpkins, with all kinds of shapes and sizes in between. Don't waste space in a very small garden growing winter squash, marrows or pumpkins, as they take up a lot of space that could be better used for growing produce that can be picked and eaten fresh. Summer squash and zucchini are generally

highly productive, with bushy or trailing habits. They are excellent for generous containers, and the trailing varieties can be trained over arches and up walls to make highly decorative summer features.

Minimum container depth: 25cm/10in
Germination period: 8-18 days
Sowing to harvest time: 9-10 weeks
Soil requirements: Very rich loam. In containers, bolster a soil-based compost with up to 30% manure. Squash will grow happily in almost pure manure.
Climate: Squashes need sun and don't fruit well in cold damp summers.
Cultivation: Sow seeds in spring on a windowsill or under glass, potting on the strongest to 20cm/8in pots and transplant when a seedling fills its pot, planting out in late spring. Water plants well in prolonged dry weather.
Watch out for: Mildew (stagnant air and insufficient moisture at roots), slugs on seedlings.
In the kitchen: Side vegetable, roasted, soups & stir-fries. Flowers are delicious fried, eaten raw or stuffed.
Varieties: Tromboncino is a vigorous climber producing tasty green courgettes with bell shaped ends, Golden Zucchini is a yellow fruited prolific but compact and reliable bush variety, Delicata spreads over the edge of a tall pot, producing good numbers of creamy peanut shaped squashes with delicious flavour.

Cucumber
Cucumis sativus
Containers
Size: Climbers 1.5-3m/5ft-10ft, bushes 60cm/2ft
Ranging in fruit size, texture, flavour and color, some cucumbers climb using tendrils, others have a bushy compact habit. Most varieties require some heat to yield well. Grow outdoor or 'ridge' varieties which include gherkins and small round 'apple' cucumbers.
Minimum container depth: 20 cm/8in
Germination period: 6-14 days
Sowing to harvest time: 12-14 weeks
Soil Requirements: Very rich loam or compost.
Climate: Frost tender, most varieties of cucumber need long warm summers.
Cultivation: Sow 2 seeds per 10cm/4in pot under glass in late spring. Pot on the strongest to 20cm/8in pot and plant out next to a support when just root-bound – you can cover the container with a cloche or similar. Feed in midsummer with liquid feed, and water well when fruits are forming. To encourage side shoots you can stop the main stem when about 7 leaves have appeared.
Pests/Diseases: Mildew, slugs on seedlings, cucumber mosaic virus.
In the kitchen: Salads or pickling.
Varieties: Burpee Hybrid is a traditional long green cucumber, Crystal Apple is an excellent trailing outdoor variety with crisp round fruits. Cornichon de Bourbonne is a good pickling variety.

Endive and Chicory
Cichorium spp.
Containers and raised beds
Size: 10-15cm x 20-30cm/4-6in x 8-12in
Endives and chicory are particularly useful as tasty winter vegetables, producing slightly bitter leaves which are delicious in salads, blanched or fresh picked. Grow Witloof chicory for forcing to produce tender chicons over winter and into early spring. Grow broad leaved endives for continuous winter cut-and-come-again salad, curly leaved endives for summer salads.
Minimum container depth: 20cm/8in
Germination period: 8-21 days
Sowing to harvest time: 12weeks, 30 weeks for chicons
Soil requirements: Rich loam or compost
Climate: Witloof chicory and broad leaved endive are frost hardy, curly leaved endive is slightly tender.
Cultivation: Sow endive on your windowsill from late spring onwards and plant in a cooler part of the garden when 4 leaves are showing. Harvest the leaves in summer – some people blanch endive leaves under an inverted container before harvesting to make them sweeter. Sow chicory straight into a deep bed or container in summer, then lift the roots in autumn, cutting off all the leaves and stacking the roots in a compost filled dustbin or large container with a lid in a cool spare room or shed. Keep light excluded and don't be tempted to peep too often and after 6 weeks you will be able to harvest pale 10-15cm/4-6in chicons.
In the kitchen: Warm & cold salads, braised vegetable.
Varieties: Cornet de Bordeaux broad-leaved endive. Moss Curled curly leaved endive, Monk's Beard and Witloof chicory.

Florence Fennel
Foeniculum vulgare var dulce
Containers and raised beds
Size: 20-30cm/8-12in tall to 1m/3ft when flowering
Florence Fennel is the swollen bulb vegetable version of the aniseed flavoured herb. Sensitive to day length, it may bolt in dry conditions, especially if sown before midsummer.
Minimum container depth: 20cm/8in
Germination period: 6-12 days
Sowing to harvest time: 8-10 weeks
Soil requirements: Rich free-draining loam or compost.
Climate: Although hardy, Florence fennel prefers a sunny and sheltered position, well mulched and protected from drying winds.

Cultivation: Sow seeds in moist compost at midsummer, thinning seedlings to about 20cm/8in apart. Fennel benefits from mulching, regular gentle watering, and feeding with liquid feed as the bulb swells.
Watch out for: Slugs on seedlings, and greenfly.
In the kitchen: Salads, stews & side vegetable.
Varieties: Sweet Florence, Précoce d'Eté.

Garlic
Allium sativum
Suitable for containers and raised beds
Size: 40-60cm/ 15-24in tall
Garlic bulbs can be grown almost anywhere in a warm garden, singly, or in groups. They grow happily in containers, interspersed with fast growing salads for maximum production, although the yield is best in a raised bed where 1m²/3ft² can produce 52 garlic bulbs, one for each week of the year! Cut growing shoots for salads.
Minimum container depth: 15cm/6in
Sowing to harvest time: 6–8 months
Soil requirements: Rich free-draining loam or compost.
Climate: There are different types of garlic to suit all but the coolest climates; many are frost hardy, though all prefer some heat and a warm summer with reasonably regular rainfall.
Cultivation: Plant single cloves 8-10cm/3-4in apart and 2.5cm/1 in deep. In some areas it is traditional to plant in early November and harvest in July; in cooler regions plant in September for a summer crop or plant in February for autumn harvest.
Watch out for: Slugs on seedlings.
Varieties: Germidour and Thermidrome are excellent cool season varieties.

Kohlrabi
Brassica oleracea var gongyloides
Good in containers and raised beds
Kohlrabi have an edible swollen stem base that tastes rather like cauliflower. Quick growing small sputnik-like 'bulbs' appear above ground, they make an ideal catch crop and can be sown successively from early spring to midsummer.
Minimum container depth: 15cm/6in
Germination period: 7-12 days
Sowing to harvest time: 8 weeks
Soil requirements: Light moisture-retentive soil.
Climate: Best for cool moist climates.
Cultivation: Sow direct into the soil 5cm/2in apart from March to July, thinning to 23cm/10in apart. Crop when approximately 5cm/2in diameter.
Watch out for: Fleabeetles, slugs on seedlings, Cabbage White butterfly
In the kitchen: Use steamed or boiled as a side vegetable or grated raw in salads.

Varieties: Logo, Quickstar, Kolibra are dwarf varieties.

Leeks
Allium porrum
Good in containers and raised beds
Size: from 10cm/4in tall
Although some varieties of leeks can get very large, for small gardens you can pick them as small gourmet "pencils" which can be dotted around in odd spaces.
Minimum container depth: 20cm/8in
Germination period: 9-21 days
Sowing to harvest time: from 28 weeks
Soil requirements: Rich loam/ compost.
Climate: Frost hardy leeks like a sunny open site, they are most successful in cool northern climates.
Cultivation: Sow seeds in short rows in spring in a large pot or raised bed, when they are 10-15cm/4-6in long, lift them and replant in prepared holes 10-15cm/ 4-6in deep, and water them in gently. Harvest from early autumn.
Watch out for: Slugs, rust.
In the kitchen: Soups, stews, stocks and stir-fries.
Varieties: King Richard, The Lyon, Musselburgh.

Lettuce
Lactuca sativa
Containers and growing bags
Everyone can grow lettuces, choosing from a huge variety of attractive colored and shaped leaves, cut-and-come-again varieties or large hearted types. There are lettuces for autumn, winter, early spring and summer cropping, all varying in color, shape texture and taste.
Minimum container depth: 10cm/4in
Germination period: 10-18 days
Sowing to harvest time: 8-12 weeks
Soil requirements: Moisture retentive loam or compost.
Climate: Lettuce are a cool weather crop, most are tender, though some varieties can stand a mild winter with protection. Provide semi-shade in hot summers.
Cultivation: Depending on variety, sow lettuce seeds straight into containers from mid-spring through to mid-autumn, cloching early and late sowings for protection, or starting them indoors. For mixed salad cut-and-come-again, sow 3-4 varieties by scattering seed in patches over the surface of a container or bag. Lettuce will not germinate in temperatures above 20°C/75°F. Keep well watered in dry weather.
Watch out for: Slugs and caterpillars, rotting in wet weather.
Varieties: Brune d'Hiver (winter hearting), Tom Thumb (compact, summer hearting), Merveille de Quatre Saisons (multi-color hearting); Oak Leaf, Lollo Rossa, Frisby (loose leaf); Red Salad Bowl, Saladini (cut-and-come-again).

Okra

Hibiscus esculentus

Containers only

Okra needs heat to grow successfully, so is ideal for containers that can be moved to the sunniest spots in a garden or indoors under protection. Grow bush varieties in Northern Europe.

Minimum container depth: 25cm/10in
Germination period: 6-10 days
Sowing to harvest time: 16 weeks
Soil requirements: Very rich loam/ compost with high potash content.
Climate: Okra is extremely tender, and is rarely very productive in Northern Europe.
Cultivation: Soak seeds for a day before sowing in warm compost (22°C/70°F). Thin when large enough to handle and plant out a single plant per container when the temperature is constantly above 20°C/65°F. Harvest when the pods are immature, soft and tender.
Watch out for: Botrytis in cold conditions.
In the kitchen: Side vegetable, soups and stews
Varieties: Clemson's Spineless and Burgundy are the most suitable for cool temperate climates.

Onions and Shallots

Allium spp.

Containers and raised beds

Don't waste space on maincrop onions in a small space, but spring and bunching onions can be grown closely together or to fill up gaps in large containers or raised beds, and shallots are particularly fast growing.

Minimum container depth: 15cm/6in
Germination period: 21 days from seed, it is best to plant sets for quick harvest
Sowing to harvest time: 6-10 months from seed; 10 weeks-4 months from sets
Soil requirements: Good free-draining loam or compost.
Climate: Onions are sensitive to daylength but varieties can be found to suit most climates, as long as it is not persistently cold and damp.
Cultivation: Plant shallot sets 15cm/6in apart or singly amongst other vegetables from January onwards, those planted in March will be ready for cropping in June/July. Sow bunching/spring onions direct in soil 4 to a hole, 5cm/2in apart, successively from spring to midsummer. If you have a raised bed plant onions as part of your normal rotation to keep soil healthy, but onions do not like nitrogen and should not follow beans.
Watch out for: Slugs, onion root fly.
In the kitchen: Salads, sauces and stir-fries.
Varieties: White Lisbon for spring/bunching onions, Golden Gourmet shallots.

Oriental Greens
Brassica rapa/Brassica juncea
Ideal for Containers and raised beds
A huge range of fast-growing tasty leafy vegetables that thrive in cooler climates, providing tasty greeens for salads and stir-fries all winter. Shallow rooting mizuna, mustards, mibuna, shungiku and other varieties can be sown in troughs and windowboxes, deeper containers and beds. They are very decorative as well as tasty, with leaves from pale green to deep red, some deeply serrated, others rounded.
Minimum container depth: 10-15cm/4-6in
Germination period: 7-12 days
Sowing to harvest time: Depends on variety, from 30 days
Soil requirements: Moisture retentive loam or compost.
Climate: Prefers cool summers and cold winters, tend to bolt in warm weather.
Cultivation: Sow seed outdoors as soon as frost is passed through to autumn for continuous cropping. Keep well trimmed and do not let them go to seed. For best results resow every six weeks through the summer. Most Oriental greens overwinter happily outside.
Watch out for: Fleabeetles in late spring and summer, slugs on seedlings.
In the kitchen: Salads & stir-fries.
Varieties: Tatsoi, Mizuna, Mibuna and Mustards, Shungiku, Oriental Saladini and Texsel Greens, PakChoi. Mixed seeds marketed under such names as Spicy Mix or Braising mix

Parsnips
Pastinaca sativa
Dwarf varieties suitable for containers, traditional varieties need raised beds
Few parsnips are suitable for small gardens as they are large vegetables with roots growing from 20-50cm/8-20in deep. However, dwarf varieties have recently been developed which are ideal for limited space.
Minimum container depth: 20cm/8in
Germination period: 21-28 days
Sowing to harvest time: 26-30 weeks
Soil requirements: Free draining sandy loam or compost.
Climate: Frost hardy, best in cool northern climates.
Cultivation: Sow direct in March 10-15cm/4-6in apart, soeing several seeds at each point – germination can be erratic as parsnip seed does not store well. Mulch after thinning and water in prolonged drought. Crop from first frost onwards through winter.
Watch out for: Carrot fly, canker.
In the kitchen: Boiling, roasting, chips.
Varieties: Lancer and Arrow are dwarf varieties.

Sweet Peppers / Chiles
Capsicum spp
Ideal for Containers
Size: 30-90cm/12-36in tall
There are a huge range of capsicums, from sweet peppers to fiercely hot chillies, but the hottest varieties will only grow in hot climates. All peppers need heat but a few sweet peppers can be grown outside successfully in warm seasons. Some small hot chillies can make excellent productive houseplants for sunny rooms.
Minimum container depth: 20cm/8in
Germination period: 14-20 days
Sowing to harvest time: 16-26 weeks
Soil requirements: Very rich compost.
Climate: Frost tender, in Northern Europe grow peppers on sunny windowsills, in conservatories or in very sunny areas of the garden.
Cultivation: Sow seeds in a tray on a warm windowsill in early spring, potting on the strongest into 5cm/2in pots when three leaves are showing. When the root fills the pot, pot on to 20cm/8in pot until almost ready to flower, (restricting the roots encourages the plant to fruit) then plant in a larger container in early summer. Peppers need gentle regular watering and benefit from regular liquid feeding. They may not color on the plants unless it is a very hot summer, so pick them green and color them off the plant in a warm room.
Watch out for: Slugs; mildew, white fly.
In the kitchen: Salads, sauces, stews and stir-fries.
Varieties: Yellow Bell, Pimento, Large Sweet Spanish, Sweet Cherry; grow Anaheim for medium hot peppers.

Peas
Pisum sativum
Containers and raised beds
Size: Climbing varieties grow to 1.2-3m/4-10ft.
Peas are not a very efficient use of space in a small garden, unless growing dwarf varieties unsupported amongst salads in successive sowings from March to July. Grow snap peas and mangetout types for eating raw, and podding varieties for eating fresh after shelling, or for freezing. Peas increase nitrogen in the soil.
Minimum container depth: 15cm/6in
Germination period: 7-20 days
Sowing to harvest time: from 12 weeks when sown in autumn, 9-11 weeks from spring sowing.
Soil requirements: Neutral compost in containers; any fertile soil in raised beds.
Climate: Peas are a cool weather crop, in warmer temperate zones sow in autumn or very early spring and crop before the heat of summer.
Cultivation: Sow directly into the compost 5-7.5cm/2-3in apart in spring, or sow under cover in autumn. Peas should

be supported by twiggy 'pea sticks', or you can twine them round poles or attach them to mesh. Harvest peas when pods are tightly filled or when mangetout pods have stopped lengthening. Pick frequently and keep well watered.
Watch out for: Sow as early as possible to avoid pea moth.
In the kitchen: Snap or mangetout peas are delicious in salads and stirfries, podded peas best steamed or boiled then eaten hot or cold.
Varieties: Kelvedon Wonder is excellent in containers. Golden Sweet, a climbing purple-flowered and lemon-yellow edible podded pea, is highly ornamental.

Potatoes
Solanum tuberosum
Ideal for large containers and stacking tubs
Size: 15-25cm/6-10in deep, or stacked up to 1m/3ft high, with foliage 30-75cm/12-30in tall.
Although potatoes are traditionally grown in deep trenches, taking up a lot of space, you can grow them very successfully in scarcely any space. Nor do you need to be restricted to growing early potatoes in small gardens as maincrop potatoes can produce high yields when grown in stacking boxes.
Minimum container depth: several 30cm/1ft stacking containers
Sowing to harvest time: 12 weeks earlies, 18 weeks maincrop.
Soil requirements: Rich moisture-retentive well-manured loam or compost.
Climate: Most varieties are slightly frost tender, though they can be grown successfully at altitude.
Cultivation: Sprout potatoes during late winter in a warm place, to produce a number of green-purple shoots of about 2.5cm/1in long. Plant earlies in a compost bag, large container, or manured bed as soon as the ground is warm – it is traditional throughout much of England to plant them on Good Friday. Late frost may burn leaves, but plants usually recover. When the foliage is 30cm/1ft tall, earth up the plants until only the top leaves show, and water & feed regularly when flowers start to show. Start cropping earlies at the beginning of summer.
Maincrop potatoes can be grown very easily over a longer season in stacking containers. Plant tubers 20cm/8in apart in spring in a bottomless container or tyre. The main shoot will produce tubers when covered. As more tubers are produced, cover them with earth and compost and stack another bottomless container on top. Stack up several containers high, filling each one with compost to just below the top of the foliage, until a month after midsummer. Water and feed the stacks regularly to maintain the moisture level. Harvest maincrop potatoes all at once at the end of summer, and store.

Watch out for: Slugs, potato blight (burn all affected plants).
Varieties: Epicure, Edzell Blue, Pink Fir Apple and Charlotte for earlies; King Edward, Dunbar Standard and Bute Blues for maincrop.

Summer Radishes
Raphanus sativus
Excellent in containers and windowboxes
Summer radishes are quick-growing and useful for catch cropping.
Minimum container depth: 10cm/4in
Germination period: 4-10 days
Sowing to harvest time: 3-6 weeks
Soil requirements: Free draining sandy compost.
Climate: Radishes do not need a lot of heat although they taste more peppery under hotter conditions. They prefer a light sunny site but will grow in semi-shade.
Cultivation: Scatter radish seeds direct into any spare patch of soil from late spring onwards every 1-2 weeks.
Watch out for: Flea beetle, birds.
In the kitchen: Salads.
Varieties: As well as conventional small round red radishes try the more substantial French Golden, French Breakfast and Long White Icicle.

Spinach
Spinacea oleracea
Containers and raised beds
15-30 x 60 cm/6-12 x 24in
Leafy green spinach is an excellent subject for container growing. Although most spinach is slightly frost tender, New Zealand spinach is perennial, can be grown in virtually any condition and is slow to bolt. True spinach tends to bolt readily in hot and dry conditions and should be grown in succession over a season to maintain yields.
Minimum container depth: 20cm/8in
Germination period: 10-20 days
Sowing to harvest time: 8-12 weeks
Soil requirements: Moist rich loam or compost.
Climate: Spinach is a cool weather crop, and needs moisture.
Cultivation: Sow spinach from April-September in patches on its own or as a 'catch', intercropping amongst other immature vegetables. Mulch young plants well and thin when they are about 8cm/3in tall, eating the thinnings in salads.
Watch out for: Slugs on seedlings, powdery mildew in dry conditions.
Varieties: Spinoza, Medania, Strawberry Spinach, New Zealand (Everlasting).

Sweetcorn
Zea mays
Containers and raised beds
Size: 1.5-2m/4^1/2-6ft

You probably wouldn't immediately think of sweetcorn for a small space, but as long as your garden is sunny you can produce a reasonable crop of full size sweetcorn from as few as 6 plants grown in a block in a deep container filled with well manured soil – and even if the harvest is small the plants are very statuesque and decorative. Or choose from the varieties of baby sweetcorn now available, although these may need more sun.

Minimum container depth: 30cm/12in for traditional varieties; 20cm/8in for baby sweetcorn

Germination period: 10-15 days in warmth over 10°C/50°F.

Sowing to harvest time: 12-17 weeks

Soil requirements: Rich previously manured loam or soil-based compost.

Climate: Sweetcorn need a long warm summer if growing unprotected in northern latitudes.

Cultivation: As sweetcorn need heat to germinate, but don't like their roots being disturbed, it is best to sow seeds in 5cm/2in biodegradeable pots or toilet roll centres in a warm place in spring, planting out in warm soil in a container when the seedling is 10-15cm/4-6in tall. Or you can sow direct into rich soil. Mulch plants well for stability. Although sweetcorn are windpollinated it is a good idea to handpollinate them by stroking the silky female tassels with pollen from the male flower that grows at the top. Harvest when silks are brown and dry.

Watch out for: Lack of pollination due to cool conditions and overdry soil.

Varieties: Minor and Mini Pop are baby sweetcorn. The most reliable full sized sweetcorn are Golden Sweet F1, and Golden Bantam. There are many attractive colored varieties, but they rarely ripen in a Northern European summer.

Tomatoes
Lycopersicon esculentum
Ideal for Containers and Growing bags
Size: from 20cm/8in to 90cm/3ft

Tomatoes come in different colors, shapes and sizes, but are usually classified as tall, indeterminate or cordon types that fruit over a long period, and bush or determinate types that crop heavily for a shorter time. Many small fruited bush types are ideal for hanging baskets and windowboxes as well as other containers.

Tomatoes need warmth and sun to ripen, and will grow as happily indoors on a sunny windowsill as in a warm spot outside.

Minimum container depth: 20cm/8in for standard types, 10cm/4in for cherry/tumbling types

Germination period: 8-16 days on a warm windowsill.

Sowing to harvest time: 16-22 weeks

Soil requirements: Rich moisture-retentive alkaline loam or compost. It is worth adding a tablespoon of ground lime to each container to reduce the acidity of most rich compost mixtures. and a handful of potash or woodash.

Climate: Tomatoes are tender and need long summers, but some types will grow in all but the coolest climates.

Cultivation: Sow seeds in trays on a sunny windowsill, planting out into 7.5cm/3in pots when at least two leaves are showing. Allow the seedlings to fill the pot completely before potting on into progressively larger containers as root constraint promotes fruiting. If you have space on your windowsill, wait to plant outside in their final containers, bags or baskets until the first flowers are showing, otherwise put out when all danger of frost is well past. Water regularly and never allow the plants to dry out, but don't overwater as this can lead to blossom end rot where fruits blacken at the blossom end as soon as they ripen. Fruits can split after heavy rain. Take off some leaves below and up to the truss when fruits begin to color to allow light and ventilation.

For tall varieties, stake as soon as they are 20cm/8in tall, nip out secondary shoots inside the elbows of branches and pinch out the growing tip in midsummer to restrict size and put energy into fruiting.

Watch out for: Mildew (stagnant air and insufficient moisture at roots), slugs, tomato mosaic virus, blight.

Varieties: Gardener's Delight and Tigerella for salads; San Marzano and Roma for plum tomatoes; Brandywine for large slicing tomatoes; Tumbling Toms for hanging baskets, Yellow Currant and Green Grape for unusual cherry tomatoes.

Turnips
Brassica rapa
Containers and raised beds
Small fast-growing turnips are excellent for containers.

Minimum container depth: 20cm/8in

Germination period: 6-14 days

Sowing to harvest time: 8-12 weeks

Soil requirements: Moist well manured loam or compost.

Climate: Cool moist climate is ideal.

Cultivation: Sow direct 5-10cm/2-4in apart in late spring or early summer, and start cropping when turnips are only 3cm/1in diameter.

Watch out for: Slugs on seedlings, flea beetle.

In the kitchen: Side vegetable, stews and grated in salads.

Varieties: Golden Ball, Snowball

SALAD GREENS

Chickweed

Stellaria medica

Containers and raised beds

A useful early salad, and good for groundcover round fruit trees and other vegetables.

Minimum container depth: 10cm/4in

Germination period: Needs a period of cold to start germination, then 4-8 days. Often appear in autumn soon after first frost.

Sowing to harvest time: Self-seeding, best to eat in autumn and early spring.

Soil requirements: Any light soil

Climate: Frost hardy

In the kitchen: Salads.

Chives

Allium schoenoprasum

Containers and windowboxes

Minimum container depth: 10cm/4in

Germination period: 8 days, but seeds must be refrigerated first. It is easiest to obtain a divided clump.

Sowing to harvest time: As little as 2-3 weeks, though seeds usually need dormant winter period before germination. Best from spring to early summer.

Soil requirements: Light moisture-retentive loam or compost.

Climate: Frost hardy, chives die down in winter.

Cultivation: Clumps can be divided and replanted in mid-spring 15cm/6in apart, or sow seeds in spring. Chives benefit from regular watering, they can be protected in pots for early and late growth. If you remove flower stems before flowering you will increase leaf productuion.

In the kitchen: Chop into salads and sauces.

Claytonia /Winter purslane

Claytonia perfoliata

Containers and raised beds

Minimum container depth: 10cm/4in

Germination period: 2-3 days after cold dormancy.

Sowing to harvest time: Sow in spring, claytonia will self-seed freely, seeds germinating after the first winter frost.

Soil requirements: Light moisture-retentive loam or compost.

Climate: This attractive fleshy-leaved salad plant is frost hardy, though benefits from coldframe protection in very cold winters.

Cultivation: Sow sparingly in autumn and plants will form an edible green carpet.

In the kitchen: Winter salad leaf.

Dandelion

Taraxacum officinale

Containers and raised beds

Source the French large leaved variety which comes true from seed, but you can also eat your own weeds!

Minimum container depth: 10cm/4in

Soil requirements: Any light soil.

Climate: Any.

Cultivation: Sow seeds sparingly in spring, then weed out all the extra plants or your garden will be quickly overrun.

In the kitchen: Blanch the leaves and use in salads like endive.

Garlic Mustard / Jack-by-the-Hedge

Alliaria petiolata

Containers and raised beds

Size: 30-60cm/12-24in

Another spinach substitute with wonderful lemon/garlic/mustard flavour.

Minimum container depth: 15cm/6in

Harvest Time: Early to mid spring.

Soil requirements: Light moisture-retentive

Climate: Cool weather plant, frost hardy but liable to bolt in hot weather.

Cultivation: Self-seeding, and grows from root runners. Grow clumps from divisions.

In the kitchen: Use as spinach, add to salads, and chop into white sauce with fish.

Good King Henry and Fat Hen

Chenopodium bonus-henricus/C. album

Containers and raised beds

Size: 30-60cm/12-24in

Often seen as a weed, this perennial spinach substitute grows very vigorously and must be used fresh as leaves wilt quickly. Immature flowering stems can be used like asparagus.

Minimum container depth: 15cm/6in

Harvest Time: Early to mid spring.

Soil requirements: Light moisture-retentive soil.

Climate: Cool weather plant, frost hardy but liable to bolt in hot weather

Cultivation: Sow outdoors April/May and thin seedlings to 30-40cm/12-14in apart. Cut down growth in late autumn.

In the kitchen: Use as spinach

Mâche / Corn Salad
Valerianella eriocarpa
Containers and raised beds
Grow this useful small dark green salad leaf all year round, cultivating as **Claytonia** above

Salad Burnet
Sanguisorba minor
Containers and raised beds
A very hardy winter salad herb with a nutty cucumber taste.
Size: 15-40cm/6-15in
Minimum container depth: 10cm/4in
Germination period: Obtain seedlings from a nursery.
Soil requirements: Any
Climate: Very hardy.
Cultivation: Plant in a sheltered semi-shady position in spring. Cut and use leaves as soon as flowers appear.
In the kitchen: Use in salads or cook for green leafy vegetable.

Sorrel
Rumex acetosa
Containers and raised beds
Size: 10-60cm/4-24in tall
This perennial herb is hardy and self seeds happily to produce masses of delicate tasting small oval green leaves, delicious in salads and in creamy sauces.
Minimum container depth: 15cm/6in
Harvest time: Early spring leaves are best.
Soil requirements: Light moisture-retentive loam/compost.
Climate: Cool, frost hardy
Cultivation: Sorrel can be grown as an annual, sown in spring and thinned to 10cm/4in apart. As a perennial, thin to 30-45cm/12-17in apart. Renew plants every 3-4 years.
Watch out for: Slugs and greenfly.
In the kitchen: Sparingly in salads, steam with spinach, excellent in soup and for sauces.
Varieties: Broad-Leaved English sorrel is better for cool, moist climates, smaller leaved French sorrel for warmer, drier conditions.

Rocket/Arugula
Eruca sativa
Ideal for containers and windowboxes
Self-seeding peppery leaved cut-and-come-again salad crop which will produce through a mild winter.
Minimum container depth: 10cm/4in
Germination period: 1 week
Sowing to harvest time: 6-8weeks
Soil requirements: Light moisture-retentive loam or compost.
Climate: Frost hardy with protection

Cultivation: Sow thinly in early spring for early summer use, or in autumn for mild winter use. Rocket may bolt if the weather gets too warm.
Watch out for: Slugs on seedlings.
In the kitchen: Salads and soups.

Winter/Land Cress
Barberea vulgaris
Containers and raised beds
Another excellent winter salad crop, with slightly peppery leaves.
Minimum container depth: 10cm/4in
Germination period: 1 week
Sowing to harvest time: 6-8weeks
Soil requirements: Light moisture-retentive loam or compost.
Climate: Frost hardy
Cultivation: Sow sparingly in late summer in moist shade. Pick leaves through winter until flowers form.
In the kitchen: Winter salads and soups.

OTHER POSSIBILITIES
Egyptian Tree Onion
Allium cepa
Containers and raised beds
Size: 20-45cm/8-18in, 20-30cm/8-12in spread
This attractive perennial onion propagates by growing bulbils at stem tips and drooping to plant them.
Minimum container depth: 15cm/6in
Germination period: 1-2 weeks from bulbil
Soil requirements: Free draining loam or compost.
Climate: A cool weather crop that is frost hardy but will survive hot dry summers.
Cultivation: Plant bulbils 15cm/6in apart in cool weather from spring to autumn.
In the kitchen: The small bulbils can be used in salads but the early green stems are useful all year round to flavour stews, soups and salads.

Rhubarb
Rheum rhubarbarum
Containers and raised beds
Size: 45-90cm/18in-3ft tall, 60-120cm/2-4ft spread.
Although not traditionally grown in small spaces, and often viewed as a fruit, rhubarb is a sweet vegetable ideal for a slightly shady or moist spot in any garden, where sun-loving vegetables won't grow. It is a delicious early spring food, and its bright red stems and huge architectural leaves make a bold statement. The leaves are poisonous, containing high levels of oxalic acid.
Minimum container depth: 30cm/12in

Germination period: Buy nursery-grown plants.
Sowing to harvest time: 2 years
Soil requirements: Rich moist loam or compost.
Climate: Hardy, dies down in winter.
Cultivation: Grow from a root division and plant in spring or autumn in heavily manured damp soil. You can force rhubarb by covering the plant with a large upturned pot or a covered pipe or chimney pot filled with straw over the winter, to produce a crop as early as March. Keep picking the stems to avoid flowering which can exhaust the plant, and mulch with a thick layer of manure every year.
Watch out for: Crown rot in waterlogged soil.
In the kitchen: Pies, puddings, preserves.
Varieties: Cawood Delight, Hawkes Champagne, Timperly Early, Early Victoria.

Sprouting Seeds
Windowsills
A wide variety of seeds can be sprouted for salads and stir-fries. Sprouting allows the vitamins and minerals within a seed to become more digestible, and provide a range of different textures and flavours.
Sowing to harvest time: from 4 days
Germination period: a few days
Cultivation: Soak seeds in warm water overnight in a glass jar. In the morning, pour off water and replace lid, or scatter seeds on sprouter tray. Rinse seeds once a day until they are the size you want. With mustard and cress, start cress 4 days before mustard so they are ready at the same time.
Varieties: Mustard & Cress, Alfalfa, Mung beans, Aduki beans, Fenugreek, Green Lentils, Chick peas.

Welsh Onion
Allium fistulosum
Containers and raised beds
Size: 15-30cm/6-12in
This family of perennial onions propagates from side shoots. It includes fast-growing Japanese bunching or spring onion which is grown from seed as an annual.
Minimum container depth: 10cm/4in
Germination period: 1 week
Sowing to harvest time: 3-5 weeks
Soil requirements: Free draining loam or compost
Climate: Cool weather frost hardy crop.
Cultivation: Plant offsets in spring for perennial onions. For spring onions, you can sow late summer to over-winter, though they can be sown from spring to autumn for year-round use.
In the kitchen: Salads, stir fries, soups
Varieties: Hikari Bunching, Ishiko Straight Leaf, Ishikura (Japanese Bunching); White Lisbon, White Knight, Savel (Spring Onions).

FRUIT
TREE FRUIT

Apples
Malus domestica
Ideal for containers and raised beds
Size: from 60cm/2ft
No plot is too small to grow apples! Dwarfing rootstocks mean that apples are ideal for container growing. The trees are very versatile, they can be trained into many different shapes, and there are more than 4,000 cultivars to choose from with a range of fruit size, color, taste, and uses. Dwarfing rootstocks can produce trees less than 1m/3ft tall, and some varieties can be grown as 40cm/15in step-over trees or compact 'poles'. Or more than one variety can be grafted onto a rootstock to provide a pollinating partner and different varieties of apple on one tree. In temperate climates it should be possible to eat a homegrown apple every day of the year with careful choice of varieties, and good storage.
Minimum container depth: 40-60cm/15-24in
Germination period: Apples do not grow true from seed, always buy named varieties.
Harvest Time: June to December
Soil requirements: Rich, free draining loam or soil-based compost. Thoroughly topdress container soil annually, then an apple tree can happily live its life in a large container such as a dustbin or a barrel.
Climate: Apple trees are frost hardy, although the blossom of some varieties may suffer from frost. Choose varieties with respect to climate as some flower later than the last frost.
Cultivation: Plant 2 year old or older trees bare-rooted in winter, keeping the graft above the soil level. Planting distance is determined by habit so pole or cordon trees can be placed 75cm/30in apart, espaliers about 3m/9ft apart, very dwarfing open trees about 1.2m/4ft apart. Always soak roots for at least an hour before planting in a generous hole with manure and bonemeal mixed with the soil. Foliar feed during fruiting, and trees benefit from a sprinkling of potash (wood ash) around their trunks. Remove all blossom and fruit in the 1st year after planting to put energy into tree.
   Prune when dormant in winter and mulch with manure around the sides of the container (avoiding the root crown if possible). All trees, particularly those growing in containers, need gentle irrigation, especially during dry spells. When fruits are small, remove the centre fruit from a heavy cluster to allow the rest to grow larger. Some heavy bearing trees may need branch supports to avoid damage.
Watch out for: Greenfly and aphids; ants and codling moth larvae – protect with grease bands reapplied each

spring; canker – make sure pruning tools are clean.
Varieties: If you are only able to grow one tree, make sure you buy a self-fertile variety; otherwise the choice depends on taste and space. It is always best to buy from a specialist fruit nursery or a local outlet as specific varieties do best in specific areas.
Whatever variety you choose, there are certain things to watch out for. Decide what size and shape of tree and whether you want early or late fruiting, early or late flowering; whether you want dessert or cooking apples, instant eating or long storage varieties.
Choose M27 or M9 dwarfing rootstocks for the best results in containers, or fans, cordons or espaliers on M26 rootstock. Pole shaped trees are usually sold under the names Ballerina or Minarette.

Cherries
Prunus avium and P. cerasus
Some varieties satisfactory in containers
Size: 1.5-6m/4^1/$_2$-20ft
Many cherries are too vigorous to be grown in a small garden, but some varieties are good for small or medium sized plots if grown as fans or dwarfing trees and protected against birds. Sweet cherries need to be grown in the sun to ripen fruit, but acid cherries are excellent for north-facing walls as long as they are not in a frost-pocket.
Minimum container depth: 45cm/18in
Harvest Time: June to August
Soil requirements: Rich, deep, free draining loam or soil-based compost. Topdress container grown trees and mulch with manure annually.
Climate: Although frost hardy you may need to cover with horticultural fleece to protect blossom and buds from late frost. Cherries will not succeed in very wet cold climates.
Cultivation: Plant dwarfing rootstock bare-rooted bush or fan trained tree in a sunny position in winter. Make sure that planting soil is well drained and manured. Prune to shape in late spring due to risk of canker. Protect from cold, drying winds, and net against birds after fruit is set. Cherries need regular irrigation during fruit ripening, especially in dry areas.
Watch out for: Cherry blackfly, caterpillars, canker, aphids, birds.
Varieties: For a small garden choose self-fertile and compact sweet cherry varieties such as Duke or Stella, or grow fan trained Morello or Nabella acid cherries for pies and preserves.

Citrus fruits
Citrus spp
Ideal for containers
Size: 30cm/12in to 2.5m/8ft
A few varieties of oranges and lemons can be grown

outside in even cool temperate areas, provided that they are overwintered in a warm bright spot inside. They are ideal for container growing, moving them out of doors on hot sunny days and returning them under glass at the end of the day. Some dwarf citrus can be grown as productive and beautifully scented houseplants in sunny rooms. Most fruits take 12 months to mature, so trees have flowers and deeply scented fruit at the same time.

Minimum container depth: 20cm/8in for dwarf plants.

Soil requirements: Rich, free draining loam or compost.

Climate: Frost tender.

Cultivation: Best grown in containers in cool temperate climates so they can be moved inside easily. Keep well mulched and feed regularly with liquid seaweed.

Watch out for: Mealybugs, aphids, whitefly, mould.

Figs
Ficus carica
Ideal for containers
Size: 1.5-5m/4^1/$_2$-18ft height and spread
Although figs are Southern Mediterranean plants, some fare very well outside in cooler areas as long as they are protected from severe frost and placed in a sunny situation.

Minimum container depth: 45cm/18in

Soil requirements: Rich, free draining loam or compost. Top dress annually.

Climate: Although some varieties are frost hardy, figs are generally grown in mild temperate and sub-tropical climates so need protection in a northern climate.

Cultivation: Figs are strong plants whose roots need to be constrained by planting in a sturdy underground container or an open container against a warm wall. If unconstrained figs put all their energy into growing huge, their roots can destroy substantial foundations but they don't fruit well. The stronger they are constrained, the more fruit they produce, without damaging the plants at all. In northern climates, the fruit takes 18 months or more to ripen and the small figs that appear at the end of one summer should be protected over winter with straw, fleece or bubblewrap.

Varieties: Brown Turkey and Brunswick are best outside in cooler areas, otherwise there are a wide variety of succulent fruits to choose from.

Mulberry
Morus nigra
Not suitable for containers
Size: 1.5-10m/4^1/$_2$-35ft (as mature standard)
If you have a small sunny garden but would like to plant one beautiful fruiting shade tree, consider a mulberry. This is not a tree for short-term rewards as it takes up to 10 years to crop initially, but this slow-growing, long-lived tree then produces delicious fruit like loganberries for many decades or even centuries.

Harvest Time: August – September.

Soil requirements: Moist but free-draining fertile loam.

Climate: Mulberries are sensitive to heavy frost and need a warm sheltered situation in a northern garden.

Cultivation: Mulberries need to be planted in rich moist soil, they can be trained as fans on sunny walls; they must be well watered at all times as they are very sensitive to lack of water and young trees die easily from drought. Summer prune fan-trained trees, winter prune others.

Varieties: Large Black, Red.

Peaches, Nectarines, Apricots
Prunus persica and P. armenica
Suitable for containers
Size: from very dwarf 1.5m/4 1/2 ft to 5m/17ft
Minimum container depth: 45cm/18in
Harvest Time: July-September
Soil requirements: Rich, free draining loam or soil-based compost.

Climate: Peaches like hard winters and dry springs. Although they will survive frost, they prefer warm climates and need long warm summers for fruit to ripen, and they should be grown against south-facing walls for best results. They will not survive persistent wet and cold. Wet springs promote the airborne disease Peach leaf curl.

Cultivation: Grow peaches, nectarines and apricots against sun-facing walls to protect early blossom.

Watch out for: Peach leaf curl is carried in moisture, it causes leaves to curl and drop, so protect trees from spring rains by constructing a temporary polythene lean-to shelter and only moving them into the open in early summer. Or place them under hanging baskets or boxes for overhead protection.

Varieties: Many peaches and nectarines are now grown on very dwarfing rootstocks such as Pixy to produce heavy crops on very miniature trees. Peregrine and Duke of York are self-fertile.

Pears
Pyrus communis
Unreliable in containers
Pears are less successful than apples in containers as there are no very dwarfing rootstocks. Also pears are slightly more tender than apples.

Minimum container depth: 60-90cm/2-3ft
Harvest Time: August – December
Soil requirements: As for Apple
Climate: Slightly milder than Apple
Cultivation: As for Apple
Watch out for: As for Apple
Varieties: Check local successful varieties – some

espaliered pears still exist in old country gardens that have been fruiting for a century. Although there are self-fertile pears, they always fruit best if there is a pollination partner nearby. Try Beurre Hardy, Concorde, or Conference.

Plums
Prunus domestica
Good in containers and beds
Plums are easy to grow, the only problem is that they flower earlier in the season than either apples or pears, so pollination can be a problem in cool springs and late frosts can destroy blossom or destroy setting fruit. There are several good self-fertile varieties. Dwarfing rootstocks are available, for containers it is best to select a very dwarfing rootstock such as Pixy.
Minimum container depth: 45cm/18in
Soil requirements: Rich, free draining loam or soil-based compost.
Climate: Frost hardy, but early setting fruit may need to be protected with fleece.
Cultivation: Buy a 2 or 3 year old bush or place a fan trained tree against a south-facing wall. Unlike other tree fruits, do not prune in winter but wait till spring after the last frost.
Watch out for: Silver leaf, canker, greenfly.
Varieties: Victoria, Early Rivers, Denniston's Superb, Early Transparent Gage. If able to grow only one tree, obtain self-fertile variety. Damsons are not suitable for containers.

Quince
Cydonia oblonga
Satisfactory in containers
Although quinces can grow into enormous trees, they will also grow satisfactorily in containers, and will fruit in quite cool summers. The spring blossom is highly scented.
Minimum container depth: 60cm/2ft
Soil requirements: Rich, free draining loam or soil-based compost.
Climate: Frost hardy, even in Northern Europe.
Cultivation: Plant 2 or 3 year old container-grown trees in winter in manured soil. Remove fruit the first year to put strength into the plant. Prune as pear in winter. Mulch generously with manure annually.
Varieties: Vranja.

CLIMBING FRUIT

Chinese Gooseberry/Kiwi Fruit
Actinidia chinensis
Containers and raised beds
Kiwi fruit are vigorous climbers but fruit only ripen in hot summers. The chief problem in a small garden is that you need a male and female plant.
Minimum container depth: 30cm/1ft
Soil requirements: Heavily manured and free draining
Climate: Fairly frost hardy but dislike cold wet situations.
Cultivation: Plant year old rooted cuttings in well drained manured soil, and train plants on very strong trellis or strained wires. Prune at about 1.5m/4$^{1}/_{2}$ft in winter to encourage the production of lateral canes, and summer prune new shoots to five leaves to promote the production of fruiting spurs. Manure well in winter.
Varieties: Abbot, Bruno, Hayward.

Grapes
Vitus spp
Difficult in containers
Grapes do not like having their roots restricted so they are tricky in containers. It is better to dig a deep hole, fill it with rich soil/compost and plant vines permanently in a sheltered south-facing spot to train up a pergola.
Minimum container depth: 45cm/18in
Soil requirements: Rich free-draining soil
Climate: Grapes do not like persistent rain but otherwise can be grown in a wide variety of climates, given a warm summer. However only a few dessert varieties will succeed out of doors in northern Europe, while they are ideal for warmer climates.
Cultivation: Plant in March or April in a generous manure-filled hole and train up a trellis, pergola or strong wires. Train strictly and prune regularly: in the first season train the main stem up a cane, removing all side shoots; in the winter cut back to about 60cm/2ft. The following season train 3 shoots up the trellis or wires, removing further side shoots. Allow the vine to branch further each year. Net fruits and start cropping the third year.
Watch out for: Botrytis, canker, aphids, wasps.
Varieties: Black Hamburg, Golden Chasselas, Siegerrebe.

Melons
Cucumis melo
Good in containers
Size: Climbs/trails 1.5-3m
Melons need warmth and in cooler climates are best grown in containers under glass although they may fruit on an open sunny walls. They need good support, strong netting or trellis, and although they have tendrils they may need additional ties (fabric strips) when fruits swell.

Minimum container depth: 20cm/8in
Germination period: 6-14 days in warmed soil
Sowing to harvest time: 14-20 weeks
Soil requirements: Very rich loam or compost. Melons are sometimes grown on rotting straw or manure for heat and nutrition.
Climate: Very frost tender, melons need long warm summers with growing temperatures above 13°C/55°F.

Cultivation: Sow 2 seeds per 10cm/4in pot under glass, pot on the strongest to 20cm/8in pot and when just root-bound plant out in a container with a support. Good irrigation significantly improves yields.
Watch out for: Mildew (stagnant air and insufficient moisture at roots), slugs on seedlings.
Varieties: Sweetheart F1; Blenheim Orange, Extra Early Nutmeg (under glass in cool areas).

BERRIES & SOFT FRUITS

Blackcurrants
Ribes nigrum
Satisfactory in containers
Size: 60-90cm/2-3ft
Sweet small black fruits, blackcurrants can be fan or cordon trained against a north or east wall, or compact bush varieties can be grown very satisfactorily in containers. Currants bear their fruit on side shoots off 2 year old or older wood.
Minimum container depth: 30cm/1ft
Soil requirements: Rich, free draining loam or soil-based compost.
Climate: Frost hardy but not for very wet, cold climates.
Cultivation: Plant 2 year old bushes in winter in 30-45cm pots, cutting shoots to 5cm/2in above ground to promote new shoots. Prune in winter to produce an open, cup-shaped bush, ensuring a succession of year-old wood. When established, cut out very old wood to stimulate new growth. Mulch with manure every winter. Currant bushes require regular watering.
Watch out for: Aphids, red spider mite, botrytis, birds.
Varieties: Wellington, Ben Lomond.

Red & Whitecurrants
Ribes rubrum
Suitable for containers
Redcurrants are rather tart while whitecurrants are more like grapes.
Minimum container depth: 30cm/1ft
Climate: Frost hardy but not for very wet, cold climates.
Cultivation: Like blackcurrants, they can be grown near north-facing walls in warm temperate climates. Grow them as blackcurrants but do not cut the plants hard back when you plant them.
Varieties: Red Lake, White Versailles.

Gooseberries
Ribes uva-crispa
Standards are suitable for containers
Gooseberries are thorny and scratchy so do not make ideal pot plants unless they are trained as tall standards, then they can be grown very productively in containers. Most varieties need sun for the fruit to sweeten.
Minimum container depth: 30cm/1ft
Harvest Time: 30cm/12in
Soil requirements: Rich, free draining loam or soil-based compost.
Climate: Frost hardy, happy in sun or semi-shade.
Cultivation: Buy standard-trained 2 or 3 year old plants and keep well watered and prune to shape each year in winter. Top dress annually with manure.
Varieties: Golden Drop, Careless.

Blackberries, loganberries, tayberries, hybrid berries
Rubus spp.
Not suitable for containers
Hybrid berries are usually crosses between raspberries and blackberries. Most blackberry relatives are too rampant for small gardens, and too untidy and vigorous for containers. They are best planted in well-manured beds and trained along wires.
Soil requirements: Rich, free draining loam or soil-based compost.
Climate: Frost hardy, need plenty of moisture, and sun to ripen fruit.
Cultivation: Plant in winter in well-manured soil in a permanent bed against a trellis or strong wires. Spread the roots well out, then cut each cane to 25cm/10in above ground. After harvest cut each old cane to the ground, and train each new cane to the support. Manure each winter, and ensure the soil does not dry out.
Varieties: Oregon Thornless blackberry, L654 thornless loganberry, Thornless Boysenberry, Tayberry.

Blueberries
Vaccinium corymbosum
Ideal for containers
Size: 120cm/4ft
Minimum container depth: 45cm/18in
Soil requirements: Moisture-retaining ericaceous compost.
Climate: Frost hardy, need warm summer to ripen fruit.
Cultivation: Unless you live in an area with very acid soil, blueberries should be grown in containers. They need moist, acid soil, and should be well watered with rainwater – not hard tap water in dry weather. Prune only to thin out unproductive stems in spring. Feed bushes annually with a handful of hoof and horn or similar.
Watch out for: Birds.
Varieties: Berkeley, Bluecrop.

Raspberries
Rubus idaeus
Autumn varieties suitable for containers
Although you can grow raspberries in containers, summer fruiting varieties are not a sensible use of space in a small garden: they fruit on year old canes, plants are not attractive for most of the year, they require support and need netting against birds. Moreover you will need a very large barrel or tub full of well manured soil. It is better to grow raspberries along wires in deep rich soil. However, autumn fruiting varieties produce fruit on new canes from August until October, they need no support and pruning is easier.

Minimum container depth: 30cm/12in
Soil requirements: Heavily manured soil-based compost.
Climate: Frost hardy, there are varieties suitable for most temperate climates, but best in wetter zones with warm summers.
Cultivation: Plant autumn-fruiting varieties in a sunny position in spring, cutting growth to within 5cm/2in of the ground. They need no support, simply cut back in winter after leaves have dropped and mulch well with manure. Keep well watered through dry periods.
Watch out for: Aphids, viruses, raspberry beetle.
Varieties: Autumn Bliss, September, Fallgold (yellow).

Strawberries
Fragaria spp.
Ideal for containers, growing bags etc
Strawberries are ideal container fruit, they can be grown in very small spaces in tubs, growing bags, even hanging baskets. On very small plots it is best to grow large fruited summer varieties in stacking containers or window-boxes.
Minimum container depth: 20cm/8in
Soil requirements: Rich, free draining loam or compost.
Climate: Frost hardy if protected with straw or fleece. Do not like cold wet climates.
Cultivation: Plant strawberry runners in August and you can harvest fruits the following summer. Spread roots out evenly, leaving the crown at soil level, and water in well. Keep fruit well watered throughout the growing season but never allow crowns to become waterlogged or they will rot. When fruiting, you may need to place straw under fruits to stop them rotting. In autumn, cut leaves off above the crown to promote new growth. Summer fruiting strawberries are the most popular, but extend the season by planting these with perpetual varieties which produce in flushes from early summer until the first autumn frosts. Cover containers with fleece or straw for winter protection.
You can plant summer fruiting varieties into a stacking container or window-box, replacing plants every 3 years: productive strawberry plants are shortlived so each year gently peg up to 5 strawberry runners from each plant in 7.5cm/3in pots to produce plants for the following year; pinch them off when established.
Alpine strawberries are usually grown from seed sown indoors previous autumn, they produce small strawberries throughout summer and autumn. Wild strawberries can be grown for ground cover, but beware, they can be very invasive and rarely fruit well.
Watch out for: Birds, botrytis, viruses on old plants, slugs love strawberries.
Varieties: Summer Fruiting: Cambridge Favourite, Royal Sovereign, Cambridge Late Pine. Perpetual: Gento, Aromel, Sans Rivale.

HERBS

Basil
Ocimum basilicum
Ideal for containers and sunny windowsills
Size: to 25cm/10in
This tender aromatic herb is an essential ingredient for Mediterranean cooking. Grow on sunny windowsills indoors and cultivate outdoors in hot dry summers.
Minimum container depth: 7cm/3in
Germination period: 5-8 days
Sowing to harvest time: from 3 weeks
Soil requirements: Well drained rich soil or compost.
Climate: Very tender, needs heat and sun
Cultivation: Although basil thrives better during the sunny months, you can sow seeds straight into moist compost in their destined containers on a warm windowsill throughout the year for indoor cultivation. Or sow seeds indoors from May onwards for planting basil outside from mid June in northern Europe. Water plants regularly throughout the season and remove flower stalks as soon as they appear to prolong leaf growth, and pinch out tops regularly to promote bushy growth. You can lift plants in late summer and pot them in 12cm/5in pots in a rich potting compost, placing them on windowsills for autumn/winter cropping.
Watch out for: Slugs and snails, overwatering, mildew in cool damp situations.
In the kitchen: Very versatile, particularly good with salads, tomatoes and pasta.
Varieties: Small leaved varieties such as Bush basil and bushy Greek basil can be easier to grow than large leaved Sweet or Purple basil. Or try Thai basil, variegated Green Ruffles or Lemon basil.

Borage
Borago officinalis
Best in raised beds, adequate in containers
Size: 90cm/3ft
This hardy annual grows very easily in cool temnperate climates. It is usually grown for the sweet, cucumber-flavoured leaves.
Minimum container depth: 20cm/8in
Germination period: 1-2 weeks, but seeds will self-seed and overwinter.
Sowing to harvest time: 8 weeks
Soil requirements: Almost any soil
Climate: Frost hardy
Cultivation: Borage germinates easily so push a few seeds into the soil in spring after the last frost. Plants will grow in moist shade as well as sunny situations.
In the kitchen: Use in fruit punches, or shred finely in salads.

Coriander

Coriandrum sativum

Size: 20-50cm x 15-25cm/8-20in x6-10in

Good in containers indoors and out

Fresh coriander leaves and seed are important for Asian, Mediterranean and Latin American cooking. Although coriander likes warmth it bolts easily in very hot summers and thrives in a sunny position in cooler, moist conditions.

Minimum container depth: 7cm/3in

Germination period: from 1 week

Sowing to harvest time: 4-8 weeks

Soil requirements: Free draining loam or compost.

Climate: Frost tender, but can be grown inside on a sunny windowsill all year round.

Cultivation: Sow seeds 1cm/¹/₂in apart regularly all year round inside, and from late spring to late summer outside. Thin through use until mature plants are 10-15cm/4-6in apart. Water regularly outside and keep picking to prevent flowering and ensure continuous supply of leaves.It bolts easily in hot periods so sow every 4 weeks through summer.

Watch out for: Slugs, aphids.

Chervil

Anthriscus cerefolium

Good in containers

Size: to 30cm/12in

Chervil is a hardy and fast growing annual herb which can be picked through the winter. It has a fine aromatic flavour rather like aniseed.

Container depth: 10cm/4in

Sowing to harvest time: 6-8 weeks

Germination period: 3-5 days

Climate: Frost hardy

Cultivation: Sow seeds outdoors in sunny or semi shady position in March and August 1cm/¹/₂ in apart and deep for year round supply.

Soil requirements: Free draining loam or compost.

In the kitchen: Add finely chopped leaves to soups, fish and egg dishes just before serving.

Dill

Containers and raised beds

Size: 60-90cm/2-3ft

Minimum container depth: 25cm/10in

Germination period: 1-2 weeks

Sowing to harvest time: 10-12 weeks

Soil requirements: Any soil

Climate: Slightly frost hardy

Cultivation: Sow dill in late spring straight into the container or raised bed, thinning the seedlings to one or two plants per pot or 25cm/10in apart as soon as possible. You may want to make successive sowings to ensure a continuous supply of fresh leaves. Dill self-seeds freely, but do not grow it too close to fennel as it is part of the same family and cross pollinates easily. Cut feathery leaves just before flowering and use fresh.

In the kitchen: Dill is an ideal accompaniment to fish dishes.

Fennel

Foeniculum vulgare

Ideal for containers

Size: up to 120cm/4ft

This tall attractive perennial has blue tinged feathery foliage and flat heads of yellow flowers. Grown for its young shoots and seeds, and for ornament, it should only be grown in a container in a small garden.

Minimum container depth: 25cm/10in

Sowing to harvest time: 2-3 months

Soil requirements: Rich, well-drained loam.

Climate: Reasonably frost hardy

Cultivation: Sow seeds in late spring, and thin to a single strong plant, or buy a nursery grown specimen.

Watch out for: Aphids.

In the kitchen: Use seeds with cabbage and in sweet dishes, shoots in soups and stews.

Varieties: Bronze fennel is an attractive purple leaved variety.

Lavender

Lavandula spp

Good in containers

There are many varieties of lavender including dwarf varieties. Mediterranean varieties such as L. stoechas are slightly less hardy than English lavender L.. angustifolia. All are ideal for container growing and can be clipped into decorative balls and cones. Though usually grown for scent, strewing and therapeutic purposes, lavender flowers are edible and lavender can be used as a flavouring.

Minimum container depth: 20cm/8in

Germination period: Obtain rooted cuttings

Soil requirements: Well drained loam or compost with added grit.

Climate: Some varieties are less hardy than others, all require sunny positions. Not for very cold, wet climates.

Cultivation: Plant in a container in free draining compost in a sunny position. Prune after flowering to stimulate denser growth, and again in late spring to shape plants.

Varieties: L. stoechas has tall fluffy white or blue spires, L. angustifolia 'Hidcote' is particularly hardy English lavender, L. 'Munstead dwarf' is small with very soft foliage. Or choose a pink variety such as L.'Loddon Pink'.

Lemon Balm

Melissa officinalis

Ideal for containers in small gardens

Size: 30-60cm/12-24in tall

This lemon-scented hardy perennial shrub should be included in a small garden as it is an important bee plant, only plant in a container or it becomes invasive.

Minimum container depth: 20cm/8in

Germination period: Obtain a rooted cutting.

Sowing to harvest time: 20cm/8in

Soil requirements: Any

Climate: Frost-hardy perennial, dies back in winter

Cultivation: Lemon balm prefers an open sunny position, but can be grown anywhere in mild climates. Prune regularly to maintain bushy habit. Water in dry weather.

In the kitchen: Leaves can be used in teas, salads, and for flavouring sauces, fish, and preserves.

Lemon Grass

Cymbopogon citratus

Ideal for containers

Size: to 1.8m/5ft

This popular lemon-scented thick stemmed grass is native to India. Grown for its tender shoots, in cooler areas it is best grown in a conservatory or greenhouse but can be planted outdoors in summer and brought inside as the weather cools.

Minimum container depth: 25cm/10in

Germination period: Buy a nursery grown plant.

Soil requirements: Free draining loam or compost.

Climate: Frost tender.

Cultivation: Plant out in early summer and keep container well watered in a very sunny spot. Bring pots indoors in winter, or keep in a frost-free greenhouse.

In the kitchen: Use the lower stem in Thai and Asian cooking.

Lovage

Levisticum officinale

Suitable for containers

Size: to 1.8m/5ft

This tall, statuesque hardy perennial is grown for its mild aniseed flavoured leaves. It is very decorative in a container, which also prevents it spreading.

Minimum container depth: 25cm/10in

Germination period: Obtain young plants, once established lovage self-seeds.

Soil requirements: Rich well drained compost or loam.

Climate: Frost hardy, though not for very cold, wet climates.

Cultivation: Place container in a sunny open position. Replace plants every 4 years. Lovage dies back in winter to leave an underground crown.

Marjoram

Origanum spp.

Excellent in containers

Size: 30-60cm/12-24in

While sweet marjoram is a half hardy annual, pot marjoram is a hardy perennial dwarf shrub which can be grown outdoors in containers or indoors where it will continue to produce leaves all winter.

Minimum container depth: 10cm/4in

Germination period: 2-4 weeks outside, 1-2 weeks inside, though usually requires a winter dormancy.

Sowing to harvest time: 6-8 weeks

Soil requirements: Free-draining loam or compost.

Climate: Mild frost hardiness, though prefers hot dry conditions.

Cultivation: Sow straight into pots on the kitchen windowsill and either leave them there or transplant some specimens to outdoor containers in a sunny position. Prune plants after flowering to maintain a bushy habit.

Watch out for: Aphids.

Varieties: Golden marjoram is an attractive golden leaved perennial variety.

Mint

Mentha spicata

Containers only

Size: to 60cm/24in

There are mints to suit all tastes, including common mint, spearmint, apple mint and ginger mint. All should only be grown in containers as they are extremely invasive in open ground.

Minimum container depth: 15cm/6in

Soil requirements: Moisture-retaining loam or compost.

Climate: Frost hardy, prefers damp climate.

Cultivation: Mint will grow from almost any piece of fresh root, but it is best to start off with a named variety from a nursery. Plant in a container in a damp and shady spot, and keep well watered.

Pests/Diseases: Rust – but it is difficult to kill mint!

Varieties: Spearmint, Peppermint, Eau-de-Cologne, Applemint, Watermint (must be waterlogged), Greek (will stand dry soil).

Parsley

Petroselinum crispum

Size: 25cm/10in

Good in containers

Parsley is a biennial plant, usually treated as an annual, though it can be overwintered successfully with protection. Flat leaved and curly headed parsley are among the most popular and versatile herbs of all in the kitchen. Flat leaved varieties tend to have more flavour and are slightly hardier and easier to grow outdoors, but curly leaved parsley is more decorative and better for indoor and windowsill growing.

Minimum container depth: 20cm/8in
Germination period: 5-10 days indoors, up to 4 weeks outdoors for curly leaved,slightly less for flat leaved.
Sowing to harvest time: 12-16 weeks
Soil requirements: Rich, free draining loam or compost.
Climate: Frost hardy with some protection
Cultivation: Soak seeds in lukewarm water for a couple of hours before sowing 1cm/¹/₂in apart and deep in moist compost or soil outdoors in a damp semi-shady position from April onwards. Or sow in pots on a windowsill at any time of the year. Parsley can be slow to germinate, so you may prefer to buy small plants. Pick parsley heads regularly for continuous supply, thinning until mature plants are 15cm/6in apart. Cover overwintering plants outdoors with straw or light compost.
Watch out for: Slugs, aphids
In the kitchen: Multiple uses from garnish to sauces.

Rosemary
Rosmarinus officinalis
Good in containers
Rosemary is a hardy perennial shrub from southern Europe grown for sweet aromatic leaves and flowers. It is very attractive when flowering, and can be clipped to specific decorative shapes. Prostrate varieties are available for clambering over the side of a container or windowbox.
Size: 30cm-1.8m/1-5ft
Minimum container depth: 20cm/8in
Soil requirements: Free draining loam or compost.
Climate: Generally frost hardy but not for very cold, wet climates.
Cultivation: Best propagated from cuttings, or obtain nursery-raised plants and plant in late spring in free-draining compost in a container in a sunny position. Prune hard or shape after flowering to encourage lower shrubby growth, otherwise plants can get too big to grow well in containers.
Varieties: Look out for white varieties, Miss Jessops is a favourite upright variety.

Sage
Salvia officinalis
Good in containers
Size: 45-60cm/11/2-2ft
Sage is a small evergreen shrub from southern Europe grown for its aromatic leaves.
Minimum container depth: 20cm/8in
Soil requirements: Free-draining loam or compost.
Climate: Frost hardy with some protection or snow. Not for very cold, wet climates.
Cultivation: Obtain nursery grown plants and plant in

containers in an open, sunny position in spring. Prune hard after flowering to maintain compact habit, otherwise sage plants can become too big to grow well in containers. Renew plants every 6 or 7 years.
Varieties: Common, Purple, White, Golden, Variegated.

Savory
Satureja spp.
Good in containers
Size: to 40cm/15in
This family includes the hardy perennials Winter Savory (*S. montana*) and Creeping Savory (*S. spicigera*) which are hardy perennials, and Summer Savory (*S. hortensis*) which is a self-seeding annual. All prefer warm positions on free-draining soils. They are excellent bee plants.
Minimum container depth: 15cm/6in
Germination period: Summer Savory 10 days from seed, otherwise obtained plants from nursery.
Soil requirements: Free draining loam or compost.
Climate: Frost hardy with some protection. Not for very cold, wet climates
Cultivation: As **Rosemary**
In the kitchen: The aromatic leaves are especially good with red meat and beans.

Sweet Bay
Laurus nobilis
Ideal for containers
Bay trees are slow-growing but can grow to large trees in the open ground. In small gardens grow them in containers clipped into pyramids, cones or lollipops (standards).
Minimum container depth: 30cm/12in
Soil requirements: Rich, well-drained loam.
Climate: Slightly frost hardy, but move bay trees into the shelter of a greenhouse or conservatory or protect well with straw-lined sacking or bubble wrap in very frosty gardens or on roofs or balconies.
Cultivation: Plant young trees in rich soil in containers, and place in Re-pot every 2-3 years. You can propagate bay easily by sowing heel cuttings into moist compost in midsummer.
Watch out for: Aphids

Sweet Cicely
Myrrhis Odorata
Containers and raised beds
Size: 60-100cm/2-3ft
This attractive perennial hardy umbellifera herb is very decorative in a container. The leaves can be used to take away tartness in fruit (and rhubarb). The whole plant has sweet aniseed fragrance.
Minimum container depth: 20cm/8in
Grow as **Lovage**

French Tarragon
Artemisia dracunculus
Good in containers
Size: to 90cm/3ft
French tarragon is a staple of French cooking. It is less hardy than Russian tarragon, but has a much better flavor. Containers need to be moved indoors to overwinter in Northern Europe, or protected from any frost.
Minimum container depth: 25cm/10in
Soil requirements: Rich, free draining loam or compost.
Climate: Not frost hardy
Cultivation: Plant nursery bought plants in containers in a sunny position, and move indoors at the first hint of frost.

Thyme
Thymus spp
Excellent in containers or cracks in paving
Thyms is a low growing spreading evergreen shrub which is strongly aromatic. There are a wide range of varieties and forms of this useful and hardy herb. Thyme will happily grow to fill cracks of walls and pavings, as long as it is in a sunny position.
Size: to 22 cm/9in
Minimum container depth: 15cm/6in
Soil requirements: Any poor free draining soil
Climate: Frost hardy, drought resistant
Cultivation: Grow thyme from cuttings or obtain nursery-grown plants. Plant in pots in a sunny position, and shelter from cold winds. Thyme will withstand drought. Plants are not long lived and should be renewed every 3-4 years as they tend to spread leaving a bare centre. Prune after flowering to promote bushy habit.
Varieties: There are dozens of varieties with different habits – clump forming, trailing or bushy, with dark green, golden or variegated leaves. All are highly scented, lemon and orange thymes are particularly notable.

144

E D I B L E   F L O W E R S

Calendula / Pot Marigold
Calendula officinalis
Good in containers
Calendula petals make a good substitute for saffron.
Size: 30-45cm/12-18in
Minimum container depth: 15cm/6in
Sowing to harvest time: 6-8 weeks
Soil requirements: Rich, free draining soil or compost.
Climate: Frost tender. Not for very cold, wet climates.
Cultivation: Self-seeding hardy annual.
In the kitchen: Cut calendula flowers mid morning and use fresh petals in salads, or crush them into a powder.

Clove Pink
Dianthus caryophyllus
Good in containers
This hardy perennial flower from southern Europe was once widely used in wine making and in the kitchen.
Size: to 45cm (18-24in) height and spread when flowering
Minimum container depth: 20 cm/8in
Soil requirements: Any free-draining soil or compost
Climate: Reasonably frost hardy.
Cultivation: Buy nursery grown stock or sow seed in late spring for next year's flowers.
Watch out for: Blackfly
In the kitchen: Use in vinegars and sauces.
Varieties: Look for old-fashioned garden pinks such as strongly scented Mrs Simpkins, or red frilled Sops-in-Wine.

Daylily
Hemerocallis spp
Good in containers
Hardy perennial bulbs, daylilies emerge in spring, and different cultivars flower from early summer until autumn.
Size: from 30-90cm/12-36in tall
Minimum container depth: 20cm/8in
Soil requirements: Rich free-draining loam or compost.
Climate: Frost hardy.
Cultivation: Plant daylilies in autumn or sping. Pale yellow varieties need 6 hours of sun a day, darker varieties are happy in part shade. All need good drainage.
In the kitchen: Flowers and buds are delicious in soups, pancakes and stirfries. Paler colors seem sweetest, flavour getting stronger and more bitter as the color darkens.

Nasturtium
Tropaeolum majus
Good in containers
This attractive and easy to grow self-seeding climbing annual has delicious peppery flowers, seeds and leaves.
Size: Climbing to 4m/12ft; or ground hugging.
Minimum container depth: 15cm/6in
Soil requirements: Prefers poor soil
Climate: Frost tender, and need sunny position to flower.
Cultivation: Easily grown from seed, taking between 6-12 weeks to flower, then flowering continuously until frost.
In the kitchen: Flowers and leaves spice up salads, pickle the seeds and use them as capers.
Varieties: Alaska is variegated, Whirlybird from cream to scarlet, Empress of India crimson with blueish green foliage.

Pansy
Viola x wittrockiana
Good in containers and windowboxes
Pansies provide color in a cool spring and autumn garden.
Size: 15-22cm/6-9in
Minimum container depth: 10cm/4in
Soil requirements: Any moist fertile soil or compost.
Climate: Pansies need cool weather.
Cultivation: Grow from seed indoors in spring or autumn, planting out as soon as frost is past.
In the kitchen: Pansy petals are mild and sweet, a colorful and tasty addition to salads and an excellent accompaniment to pasta dishes.

Rose
Rosa spp
Satisfactory in containers
Roses have a long history of culinary, medicinal and cosmetic uses. The petals of most roses can be used.
Size: Choose roses with a fairly compact habit for container growing. If growing a climber choose a fairly slow growing one that reaches no more than 4m/12ft..
Minimum container depth: 30cm/12in
Soil requirements: Extremely rich well drained soil.
Climate: Roses are generally frost hardy but need to be placed in a sunny position and protected in cold winters by mounding straw or compost around their crowns.
Cultivation: Plant cuttings or nursery-grown stock in a container filled with manure-laden compost and place some bonemeal around the roots. The larger the container, the richer the soil, the better. Feed them throughout the growing season and top dress with manure in autumn. Roses grown in containers need to be pruned hard in autumn.
Watch out for: Slugs, aphids, black spot – but never use chemicals on food plants!
In the kitchen: Use rose petals in salads, desserts and vinegars.

RESOURCES

CONTAINER DEPTHS
AT A GLANCE

You can grow nearly anything in a container if you provide plants with suitable compost, a good situation, and plenty of water and general care. Use this handy instant reference to check what depth container you need, and return to Chapter Three for more information.

Asparagus
45cm/18in

Beetroot
Dwarf varieties only:
25 cm/10in

Beans – French/runner beans
20cm/9 in

Beans – dwarf & bush beans
15cm/6in

Broad Beans
20cm/8in

Broccoli, Calabrese & Cauliflower
Dwarf varieties only:
25cm/10in

Cabbage & Kale
Dwarf varieties only:
20cm/8in

Carrots
20cm/8in

Celery & Celeriac
Not good in containers

Chard / Leaf Beet
20cm/8in

Cucumber
20 cm

Egg Plants
20cm/9in

Endive & Chicory
20cm/8in

Florence Fennel
20cm/8in

Garlic
15cm/6in

Kohlrabi
15cm/6in

Leeks
20cm/8in

Lettuce
10cm/4in

Okra
25cm/10in

Onions & Shallots
15cm/6in

Oriental Greens
10-15cm/4-6in

Parsnips
Dwarf varieties only:
20cm/8in

Sweet Peppers / Chillies
20cm/8in

Peas
15cm/6in

Potatoes
Several 30cm/1ft stacking containers

Radishes
10cm/4in

Spinach
20cm/8in

Sweetcorn
Traditional varieties
30cm/12in; dwarf 20cm/8in

Tomatoes
20cm/8in

Turnips
20cm/8in

Zucchini & Summer Squashes
25cm/10in

SALAD GREENS

Arugula
10cm/4in

Chickweed
10cm/4in

Chives
10cm/4in

Claytonia /Winter purslane
10cm/4in

Dandelion
10cm/4in

Garlic Mustard / Jack-by-the-Hedge
15cm/6in

Good King Henry & Fat Hen
15cm/6in

Mâche / Corn Salad
10cm/4in

Salad Burnet
10cm/4in

Sorrel
15cm/6in

Winter/Land Cress
10cm/4in

OTHER POSSIBILITIES

Egyptian Tree Onion
15cm/6in

Rhubarb
30cm/12in

Welsh Onion
10cm/4in

TREE FRUITS

Apples
40-60cm/15-24in

Cherries
45cm/18in

Citrus fruits
Dwarf varieties 20cm/8in

Figs
45cm/18in

Mulberry
Not suitable for containers

Peaches, Apricots & Nectarines
45cm/18in

Pears
Unreliable in containers

Plums
45cm/18in

Quince
60cm/2ft

CLIMBING FRUIT

Chinese Gooseberry/Kiwi Fruit
30cm/1ft

Grapes
45cm/18in

Melons
20cm/8in

SOFT FRUIT

Blackcurrants
30cm/1ft

Red & Whitecurrants
30cm/1ft

Gooseberries
Standards: 30cm/1ft

Blueberries
45cm/18in

Raspberries
Autumn varieties only:
30cm/12in

Strawberries
20cm/8in

Blackberries, loganberries, tayberries
Not suitable for containers

HERBS

Basil
7cm/3in

Borage
20cm/8in

Coriander
7cm/3in

Chervil
10cm/4in

Dill
25cm/10in

Fennel
25cm/10in

Lavender
20cm/8in

Lemon Grass
25cm/10in

Lemon Balm
20cm/8in

Lovage
25cm/10in

Marjoram
10cm/4in

Mint
15cm/6in

Parsley
20cm/8in

Rosemary
20cm/8in

Sage
20cm/8in

Savory
15cm/6in

Sweet Bay
30cm/12in

Sweet Cicely
20cm/8in

French Tarragon
25cm/10in

Thyme
15cm/6in

FLOWERS

Calendula / Pot Marigold
15cm/6in

Clove Pink
20 cm/8in

Daylily
20cm/8in

Nasturtium
15cm/6in

Pansy
10cm/4in

Rose
30cm/12in

COMPANIONS
AT A GLANCE

All crops benefit from companion herbs and flowering plants to attract insect predators and deter others, and marigolds *(Tagetes)* to kill nematodes and deter some insect pests. Specific companions may also prevent diseases and deter weeds.

CROP	GOOD COMPANION	
Asparagus	Basil, tomato	**Do not** plant beans beside onions and garlic
Beans	Carrot, squash, sweetcorn	
Beetroot, spinach, chards	Onions and garlic	
Carrot	Chives, leek, lettuce, garlic, tomato	**Do not** plant carrots beside dill or fennel
Egg plant	Beans	
Kohlrabi	Beetroot and chards	
Leek	Carrot, onions and garlic	**Do not** plant squash beside potatoes
Lettuces	Dill and all annual herbs	
Onions and garlic	Beetroot, chards, lettuce. strawberry	
Pea	Beans, carrot, squash	**Do not** plant onions beside beans and peas
Radish	Lettuce, squash	
Squash/Zucchini	Beans, nasturtiums, sweetcorn	
Strawberry	Lettuce, beans, spinach	**Do not** plant tomatoes beside potatoes
Sweetcorn	Beans, squash, peas	
Tomato	Asparagus, basil, carrot, onions and garlic	

147

THE AUTHOR'S GARDEN

Our food growing adventures began when we became proud owners of a tiny plot attached to our home on a small suburban estate in North London. When we moved there the back garden was entirely covered with paving with just a few inches of bare earth on two sides, with conventional bare lawn at the front and side of the house.

Although it looked barren and rather uninviting, my partner and I realized that this garden would give us a golden opportunity to test the theories of permaculture in a small urban space. Permaculture is a design system for sustainable human habitats (*see page 24*) . We decided that, with good planning and design, we should be able to get enough fruit and vegetables from our small garden to avoid buying any through summer and early autumn. We also decided to find as many ways as possible to recycle household waste in our garden environment.

The paved area at the back was an obvious place to start. Our first step was to remove the paving slabs and upturn them as edges for raised beds, cementing them together. We chose raised beds for the ease of growing a wide range of fruit and vegetables in the first season The shape, size and position of the beds was almost predetermined as the east side of the back garden was the only area to get direct sunlight for most of the day. So we filled the space with three beds with slots between allowing free access for a person with a small wheelbarrow.

We hired a small cement mixer and spent one weekend mixing coir peat substitute, local manure, sand and any old top soil we could find. We also built a wooden compost bin from an old wardrobe. And we built a small pond from a large flower pot and attracted a fat friendly frog that stayed all summer. The first summer and autumn we succeeded with lettuce, Swiss chard, radishes, tomatoes, mange tout, Oriental greens, runner beans, potatoes, blackberries, blackcurrants, leeks, carrots, parsnips, zucchini, squash and a wide variety of herbs.

The second year we increased the growing area, the diversity, and the yields. We used old railroad ties to demarcate keyhole beds (outlined on the plan) in the back garden. With sleepers and old paving slabs we raised a plinth at the north end of the garden for a tiny lean-to greenhouse. We built a large hot box over the compost bins to

149

grow winter greens and herbs. After we have
used the previous year's compost we fill the
bins with fresh horse manure and straw,
wetted with urine and water; this builds up
heat to warm the hotbox above.

A single water barrel proved too small for
our needs the first summer. Subsequently we
built a bunker in the southeast corner of the
back garden where we store compost for
filling our potato tires, using bits of leftover
railway sleepers and plywood. This supports
a larger water tank which fills from the roof
we share with our neighbours. The old water
barrel is now used for comfrey and nettle
tonic production, an important source of
nutrients to our intensively cropped soil –
which is now a good loam! We bought a
proprietary worm bin for our kitchen waste
which produces a wonderful liquid feed as
well as compost.

As well as a wide range of annual
vegetables we have perennial herbs, greens
and fruit. A fan trained Morello cherry grows
against the west fence and at the north end of
the garden, facing south, we planted two
kinds of raspberries, blackcurrant, various
fruit and nut trees and a fantrained
greengage. Beneath them grows wild celery, autumn
raspberries, mints, Mitsuba and lemon balm. Strawberries
provide ground cover.

At the other end of the garden adjacent to the bunker water
tank we built an arbor of posts and trellis. We are training a
clematis, fragrant rose and tayberry up the support with a white
and red currant alongside. The arbor also acts as a vertical
space for hanging baskets of strawberries, trailing tomatoes and
beans. In addition there is an insect-attracting shrubbery
dominated by a small Buddleia and fragrant flowers. This
provides nectar to predators and rids us of greenfly.

150

We have now developed the front and side garden areas, much to the neighbors' surprise. Inside new paths we have built raised beds and planted more dwarf apple trees. Beds contain diverse plants including garlic, onions, runner beans, salads, broad beans and courgettes.

It has been a steep learning curve, but enjoyable, and we continue to learn. Almost everything in our garden within reach is edible. We hope that our idea of a little Garden of Eden could be an inspiration to anyone who has thought about growing food in a tiny environment. It really is possible. So, whatever your space, get out there and get growing!

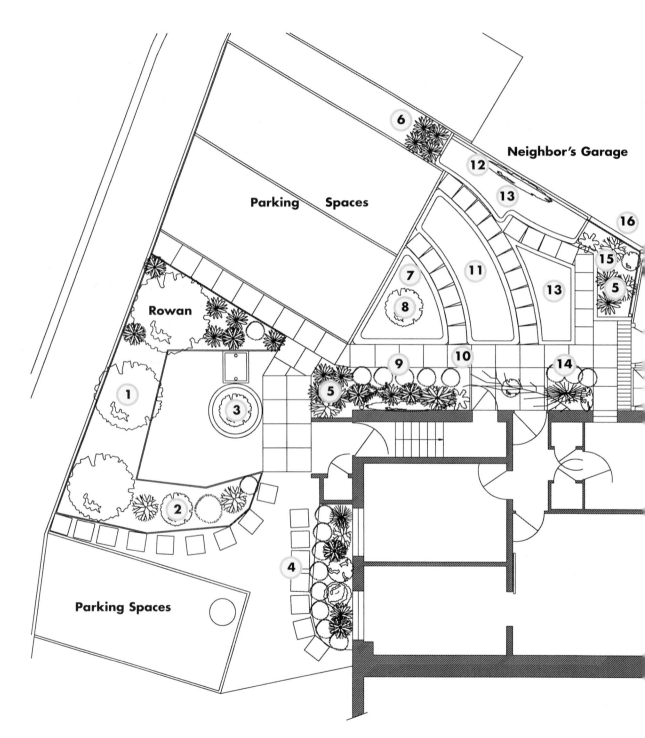

1 *Fruit & nut tree/Perennial onions*
2 *Concorde Pear/Blackcurrants/Herbs*
3 *Self-fertile Cox/Strawberries*
4 *Hot dry Herb bed*
5 *Comfrey*
6 *Horseradish*
7 *Salad Greens*
8 *James Grieve Apple*
9 *Herbs*
10 *Brown Turkey Fig*
11 *Rotation Bed 2*
12 *Fan Conference Pear*
13 *Rotation bed 1*
14 *Climbing Rose/Herbs*
15 *Redcurrants/Blackberry/Loganberry*
16 *Pole Plum*
17 *Water butt*
18 *Water tank*

19 *Hot/Compost box*
20 *Rhubarb/Mints/Honeysuckle*
21 *Small pond*
22 *Tayberry/Japonica Quince/Rhubarb*
23 *Stacking Potato box*
24 *Strawberry tower*
25 *Fan Morello Cherry*
26 *Rotation bed 3*
27 *Pollen shrubs/Nettles*
28 *Comfrey tub*
29 *8-off Cordon Apples*
30 *John Downie Crab Apple*
31 *Rotation bed 4*
32 *Raspberries/Blackcurrant/Wild Strawberry/Herbs*
33 *Lean-to greenhouse*
34 *Pole Plum*
35 *Fan Oulins Golden Gage*

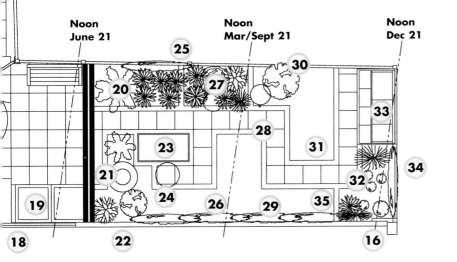

Noon
June 21

Noon
Mar/Sept 21

Noon
Dec 21

PLANT LIST

PERENNIALS INDICATED ON PLAN pp152–3

Lemon Basil
Ocimum citrodorum
Neapolitan Basil
Sweet Basil
Ocimum basilicum var neopolitana
Bush Basil   *Ocimum basilicum*
Borage   *Borago officinalis*
Caraway   *Carum carvi*
Chervil   *Anthriscus cerefolium*
Coriander
Coriandrum sativum
Dill   *Anethum graveolens*
Fennel   *Foeniculum vulgare*
Parsley   *Petroselinuim crispum*

PERENNIAL HERBS
Angelica 9
Angelica archangelica
Lemon balm 32
Melissa officinalis
Sweet bay   *Laurus nobilis* **4**
Calamint   *Calamentha nepeta* **4**
Catmint   *Nepeta cataria* **4**
Chamomile 7
Chamaemelum nobile
Chive   *Allium schoenoprasum* **7**
Garlic chive **7**
Allium tuberosum
Clary sage   *Salvia sclarea* **4**
Comfrey   *Symphytum officinale* **5**
Costmary 14
Chrysanthemum balsamita
Feverfew 9
Chrysanthemum parthenium
Horseradish 6
Armoracia rusticana
Hyssop   *Hyssopus officinalis* **9**
Lady's bedstraw 32
Galium verum
Lady's mantle 32
Alchemilla mollis
Lavender 4
Lavandula angustifolia
Lavender 4
Lavandula **'Hidcote'**
Cotton Lavender 4
Santolina chamaecyparissus
Lovage   *Levisticum officinale* **15**
Marjoram 9
Origanum marjorana

Pot Marjoram 9
Origanum vulgare
Apple Mint 20
Mentha suaveolens
Ginger Mint 20
Mentha x gentilis
Peppermint 20
Mentha x piperita
Pineapple mint 32
Mentha rotundifolia
Spearmint   *Mentha spicata* **32**
Oregano   *Oreganum variegata* **9**
Rosemary 4
Rosmarinus officinalis
Rosemary 4
Rosmarinus **'Miss Jessop'**
Rue   *Ruta graveolens* **9**
Sage   *Salvia officinalis* **4**
Purple sage 4
Salvia purpurescens
Mountain Savory 4
Satureja repanda
Summer savory 4
Satureja hortensis
Winter savory 4
Satureja montana
Soapwort 32
Saponaria officinalis
Southernwood 32
Artemisia abrotanum
Sweet cicely 9
Myrrhis odoratus
Tansy   *Tanacetum vulgare* **9**
Tarragon 4
Artemisia dranunculus
Thyme   *Thymus vulgaris* **9**
Lemon thyme 9
Thymus citrodorus
Creeping thyme PATHS
Thymus serpyllum x album
Yarrow   *Achillea millefolium* **4**

SALAD GREENS
Dandelion 7
Taraxacum officinale
Wild celery 32
Apium graveolens
Endive 7
Good King Henry 7
Chenopodium Bonushenricus
Indian mustard 7

Lambs lettuce 7
Valerianella eriocarpa
Land cress 7
Marigold   *Tagetes minuta* **7**
Nasturtium 7
Tropaeolum majus
Japanese parsley 32
Cryptotaenia japonica
Rocket   *Eruca sativa* **7**
Salad cress 7
Sorrel   *Rumex acetosa* **7**

ANNUAL VEGETABLES
predominantly in rotation beds
11,13,26,31
Aubergine   (Short Tom)
Broccoli   (Purple sprouting)
Brussels sprouts
(Cor Valient F1)
Cabbage   (Minicole)
Carrot   (Autumn King)
Carrot   (Chantenay red cored)
Carrot   (Early Nantes)
Caulliflower   (Garant mini)
Chicory   (Sugar loaf)
Chicory   (Witloof)
Chinese cabbage
(Jade Pagoda)
Chinese cabbage
(Tip Top F1)
Chinese cabbage
(Wong Bok)
Chrysanthemum greens
(Shungiku)
Courgette   (Green Bush)
Courgette   (Gold Rush)
Cucumber   (Crystal apple)
Fava Beans   (Express)
Flageolet Beans   (Chevrier Vert)
French Beans
(Blue Lake - climbing)
Japoanese burdock
Kale   (Thousand head)
Kohl Rabi   (Purple Vienna)
Kohl Rabi   (White Vienna)
Leek   (Argenteuil)
Leek   (St Victor)
Lettuce   (Little Gem)
Lettuce   (Lolla Rossa)

Lettuce (Saladini)
Lettuce (Webbs)
Mangetout peas
(Sugar snap)
Marrow (Custard)
Melon (Sweetheart)
Mizuna
Onions (Florence)
Onions (James Long Keeping)
Onions (Senshuyu)
Onions (Giant Zittau)
Oriental greens (Tatsoi)
Parsnip (White Gem)
Pak Choi
Pepper (Ethiopian)
Pepper (Hot Wax)
Pepper (Serano)
Potatoes (King Edward) 23
Potatoes (Rocket) 23
Radish (French Breakfast)
Radish (Icicle)
Radish (Mooli)
Rhubarb chard

Runner bean (Red Knight)
Runner bean (Desiree)
Spinach (Medania)
Squash (Butternut)
Sweet Corn (Morning Sun F1)
Swiss chard
Tomato (Gardeners Delight)
Tomato (Nova)
Tomato (Super Marmande)
Tomato (Whippersnapper)
Spaghetti Squash
Welsh onion

FRUIT
Apple (James Grieve) 8
Apple (Jonagold/Suntan/Gloucester 69/Crawley Beauty/ Edward VII/ Court Pendu Plat) 29
Blackberry 15
(Oregon Thornless)
Blackcurrant 12/32
(Ben Lomond)
Cherry (Morello) 25

Crabapple (John Downie) 30
Fruit and Nut 1
(Victoria plum/Sweet almond/Dennistons Gage)
Gooseberry 32
Greengage (Oulins Golden) 34
Loganberry 15
(LY 654 Thornless)
Pear (Conference) 2
Raspberry (Autumn Bliss) 32
Raspberry (Glen Prosa) 32
Redcurrant (Laxtons No 1) 22
Rhubarb (Cambridge) 20
Rhubarb (Cawood Delight) 15
Strawberry (Bounty) 24
Strawberry (Dutch) 24
Strawberry (Elisanta) 24
Strawberry (Rhapsody) 24
Tayberry 22
White currant 22
(White Versailles)
Wild strawberry 32/12

BIBLIOGRAPHY

DESIGN

Permaculture - A Design Manual, Bill Mollison, Tagari, 1994
For those who wish to get further into sustainable landscape design, from the design of windowboxes through to planets!

How to Make a Forest Garden, Patrick Whitefield, Permaculture Resources, 1996
An excellent manual for temperate forest gardens.

Designing and maintaining your Edible Landscape Naturally, Robert Kourik, Metamorphic Press, California, 1986

Urban Permaculture, David Watkins, Permaculture Resources, 1993
A good compact volume on designing for an alternative urban lifestyle.

VEGETABLES

The Salad Garden, Joy Larkcom, Penguin, 1996
The classic text on growing a huge range of year round salads. Includes recipes.

Oriental Vegetables, Joy Larkcom, Kodansha International, 1994
The definitive guide to an enormous variety of tasty vegetables.

Heirtloom Vegetables, Sue Stickland, Fireside1997
An informative and colorful guide to our vegetable heritage. Gives details of old and rare varieties, where to find them and how to grow them.

Vegetables (The Random House Garden), Roger Phillips and Martyn Rix, Randolph Press, 1993
An illustrated encyclopedia of vegetables from around the world.

Bibliography

Herbs, Roger Phillips and Nicky Foy, Pan, 1992
From the Phillips/Pan photographic reference series, includes herbs for every conceivable use.

APPLES

The Book of Apples, Joan Morgan and Alison Richards, Ebury Press, 1992
A definitive history on the most versatile of fruit. Includes a directory of the 2000+ apple species in the National Fruit Collection at Brogdale, Kent.

FLOWERS

Edible Flowers - from Garden to Palate, Cathy Wilkinson Barash, Fulcrum, Colorado, 1993
A good combination gardening guide and cookbook focusing on the most popular and widely used edible flowers

GENERAL

Companion Gardening, Bob Flowerdew, Kyle Cathie, 1993
A good commonsense guide to companion planting.

The Natural Garden, Peter Harper, Fireside, 1993
Good general guide to natural gardening, from growing food to providing wildlife havens.

PHOTOGRAPH CREDITS

Iain Bagwell 5, 24, 45, 56, 67, 96
David Cavagnaro 36, 73, 75
Jo Fairley 111, 112
Michael Guerra 148(3), 149, 151
John Hodder 46
Saxon Holt 20, 27, 41, 79

Marianne Majerus 10, 14, 30, 57, 59, 88, 91, 98, 118
Sarah McGibbon 76, 77, 86, 87
Maggie Oster 17, 18, 23, 29, 34, 35, 40(2), 51, 54(3), 61, 63, 64, 68(3), 70, 84, 93, 116

David Pearson 103
Charlie Ryrie 13, 55, 78
Steve Teague 2, 7, 39, 52(2), 55, 94, 105, 115
Linda Yang 15, 74, 81, 85, 89, 101, 109, 110

PUBLISHER'S ACKNOWLEDGMENTS

Thanks primarily to the author for his patience and understanding as we asked him to add more and more, and to his wife Julia who helped add, check and type even when just about to produce twins!
Thanks to Highfield Nursery, Whitminster, Gloucester, for supplying lots of containers, plants and space for photography, particularly Joan, Stella and Trevor. Thanks to Yolande at Bookwork for endless patience and a ready smile. Thanks to Beth at Gaia, Stroud, for all her photocopying and running around. Thanks to Jill Ford for indexing swiftly and efficiently.

I N D E X

Index